# USA TODAY

## Lifeline

### BIOGRAPHIES

# HILLARY RODHAM CLINTON

## Secretary of State

### by JoAnn Bren Guernsey

Twenty-First Century Books · Minneapolis

HILLARYCLINTON.COM

Twenty-First Century Books
A division of Lerner Publishing Group, Inc.
241 First Avenue North
Minneapolis, MN 55401 U.S.A.

Website address: www.lernerbooks.com

The publisher wishes to thank Phil Pruitt and Ben Nussbaum of USA TODAY for their help in preparing this book.

Library of Congress Cataloging-in-Publication Data

Guernsey, JoAnn Bren.
    Hillary Rodham Clinton : secretary of state / by Joann Bren Guernsey.
       p.   cm. — (USA today lifeline biographies)
    Includes bibliographical references and index.
    ISBN 978-0-7613-5122-1 (lib. bdg. : alk. paper)
    1. Clinton, Hillary Rodham—Juvenile literature. 2. Presidents' spouses—United States—Biography—Juvenile literature. 3. Women legislators—United States—Biography—Juvenile literature. 4. United States. Congress. Senate—Biography—Juvenile literature. 5. Women presidential candidates—United States—Biography—Juvenile literature. 6. Women cabinet officers—United States—Biography—Juvenile literature. I. Title.
    E887.C55G843 2010
    973.929092—dc22 [B]                                         2009011725

Manufactured in the United States of America
1  2  3  4  5  6  –  PA  –  15  14  13  12  11  10

## USA TODAY Lifeline BIOGRAPHIES

**Former rivals:** Barack Obama *(right)*, shown here with Hillary Rodham Clinton at a campaign event in 2008, asked Hillary to be his secretary of state after he was elected president.

# A New Job

Senator Hillary Rodham Clinton faced a big decision in late 2008. After a historic but ultimately unsuccessful run for the Democratic Party's nomination for president, she had been asked by Barack Obama, the new president-elect, to become U.S. secretary of state. She had been in the political spotlight for thirty years, as the First Lady of Arkansas, the First Lady of the United States, and as a U.S. senator from New York.

Discussions—and press leaks—about Hillary being offered the job started in mid-November. But

Hillary's husband, former president Bill Clinton, his foundation, and his annual Clinton Global Initiative (CGI) meetings took the limelight. The Clinton Foundation gets donations from around the globe, including from foreign governments. The former president also makes considerable money for his foundation through speaking engagements at home and abroad. He also directs the CGI.

Critics suggested that a conflict of interest would exist for Hillary if Bill continued to meet with and get money from foreign governments. They felt outsiders might confuse Bill's messages with Hillary's. As a result of these concerns, Obama's transition team began meetings with the former president. Together, they devised a way to allow Bill Clinton to continue his work on such issues as HIV/AIDS and global warming, while making sure his foundation and the CGI offered no ways for him to appear to be speaking for the United States. The former president agreed to identify all present and future donors. He spun off the CGI to be a separate entity and stopped it from accepting donations from foreign governments. In the future, he will only host the CGI meetings, not direct them. He also agreed to submit his speaking schedule for review.

Meanwhile, Hillary thought through the pros and the cons. To take the job of secretary of state meant Hillary would give up her position in the Senate and would align herself with Obama, against whom she'd fought a spirited campaign. Many thought this alignment might stop Hillary from making another run for the presidency later on. Others felt being secretary of state would show off her skills as an executive and as a foreign policy negotiator—skills that would only enhance her reputation as a potential president. Still others continued to worry about how Bill Clinton would help or hinder her as the Obama administration's chief foreign policy official.

Many Hillary supporters said she was highly qualified for the job. During Bill Clinton's presidency, she had met with famous world leaders. As a U.S. senator, she'd served on armed services and environment committees that dealt with U.S. and international affairs. She had broad-based support among Americans and had proven her commitments to international issues such as women's rights and climate change. People who had worked hard to elect Obama weren't so sure, however. Hillary had harshly criticized Obama's lack of experience during the campaign. They wondered if she would bring her message—or Obama's—to foreign leaders.

President-elect Obama wanted to pull together a "team of rivals"—highly intelligent and forceful advisers—to ensure that new ideas were being put forth to solve the country's ongoing and thorny international challenges. That's why he offered Hillary the job of secretary of state. She agreed to take it on November 21, 2008, pending a Senate confirmation hearing.

The first hearing took place in early January in front of the members of the Senate Foreign Relations Committee. Because Hillary was a senator, she knew most of the committee members very well. The senators questioned her about her vision for the State Department, about her stance on a wide variety of foreign policy issues, and about her husband's foundation. Hillary responded thoroughly to every inquiry.

**Confirmation hearing:** Hillary listens to a question from a senator during her confirmation hearings for secretary of state in January 2009. Her daughter, Chelsea Clinton, sits behind her.

## January 13, 2009

# Clinton's State hearings begin

<u>From the Pages of<br>USA TODAY</u>

Hillary Rodham Clinton debuts today as Barack Obama's choice for secretary of State in what Republicans say should be a largely friendly Senate Foreign Relations Committee confirmation hearing.

"Eight years in the Senate, eight years as first lady, she's had a lot of international experience," said Republican Sen. Johnny Isakson of Georgia, a committee member who sees no impediment to her quick confirmation as the nation's top diplomat.

Although the New York senator is likely to face little opposition among colleagues when the hearing begins at 9:30 a.m., she confronts bracing challenges in her new job. The litany of U.S. foreign policy challenges is well-known: winding down the war in Iraq while intensifying the fight against extremists in Afghanistan and Pakistan; slowing Iran's nuclear program; managing the Israeli-Palestinian conflict amid a war in Gaza, to name a few.

What gets less attention is the extent to which many experts feel the State Department is ill-equipped to carry out its mission. In October, a report by the American Academy of Diplomacy and the Henry L. Stimson Center concluded that "our foreign affairs capacity is hobbled by a human capital crisis. We do not have enough people to meet our current responsibilities." "The contrast, I think, is quite stunning," said former secretary of State Madeleine Albright, who expects Clinton to discuss the gap at today's hearing.

"She's really enthused about this job," said Sen. Robert Casey, D-Pa., a committee member who met with Clinton on Friday. "I've just noticed a change in her." There are reasons to be optimistic about Clinton's prospects for success, said James Lindsay, director of the Robert S. Strauss Center for International Security and Law at the University of Texas' LBJ School of Public Affairs. "She is a battle-tested political veteran," he said. "She's seen life from the White House. She's seen life from the U.S. Senate. She has traveled much of the world. She can command respect. She has demonstrated that she can handle tough times."

—Ken Dilanian

She recognized, for example, that running the State Department operationally and meeting with world leaders were both important and time-consuming jobs. She told the members that, if confirmed, she intended to appoint two deputy secretaries of state—one to handle management of the thousands of State Department personnel and another to improve training of those workers. She also let the members know she was reviewing the department's various financial aid efforts under the U.S. Agency for International Development (USAID) program.

Hillary reiterated her commitment to issues she'd been supporting for many years. She added her commitment to a host of other goals, including nuclear nonproliferation and energy independence. She also echoed the use of "smart power"—the combined and balanced use of diplomacy, development aid, and defense strategies—to achieve U.S. goals. In addition, she reminded the senators that she wanted to spearhead a bipartisan dialogue within the Senate by meeting often with the Foreign Relations Committee. She also mentioned she was looking forward to cooperating, rather than competing, with the U.S. Department of Defense.

To questions about the Clinton Foundation, Hillary answered that the decisions hammered out between Bill and the Obama transition team were sufficient to make sure no conflict of interest existed. Following more confirmation hearings, a majority of the committee recommended that she be confirmed. The full Senate voted 94–2 in favor of confirmation on January 21, 2009, and she was sworn in the next day. That day Hillary Rodham Clinton started a new chapter of her interesting, challenging, and uniquely varied life.

Two Republican members of the Senate Foreign Relations Committee—Jim DeMint of South Carolina and David Vitter of Louisiana—voted against Hillary's confirmation.

**Hillary's home:** Hillary grew up in this house in Park Ridge, Illinois, a suburb of Chicago. She lived here with her parents, Hugh and Dorothy, and her brothers, Hugh Jr. and Anthony.

# A Young Activist

Hillary Diane Rodham was born on October 26, 1947, at Edgewater Hospital on the North Side of Chicago, Illinois. She grew up in a stone-and-brick house on the corner of Wisner and Elm streets in Park Ridge, a middle-class Chicago suburb.

Her father, Hugh Rodham, had started his career as a curtain salesman at the Columbia Lace Company in Chicago. Dorothy Howell Rodham, Hillary's mother, met Hugh when she applied for a secretarial job at the company in 1937. Dorothy and Hugh were married in 1942. After serving in

Hillary's birth date puts her under the Zodiac sign of Scorpio. People under this sign are described as loyal, competitive, determined, and passionate, with penetrating intelligence.

the navy during World War II (1939–1945), Hugh Rodham opened his own drapery-making business, Rodrik Fabrics, in Chicago.

Like most women of this era, Dorothy stayed home to raise children. Hillary had two younger brothers: Hugh Jr., born three years after Hillary, and Anthony (Tony), born four years after Hugh. Dorothy was proud of her work as a full-time housewife and mother. Hillary remembers her as a "woman in perpetual motion, making the beds, washing the dishes, and putting dinner on the table precisely at six o'clock." At the same time, Dorothy developed and passed on to her children what would later be called feminist ideals. She said, "I was determined that no daughter of mine was going to have to go through the agony of being afraid to say what she had on her mind." Hillary added, "My parents gave me my belief in working hard, doing well in school, and not being limited by the fact that I was a little girl."

**Toddling along:** Hillary, shown here in 1950, spent a lot of time with her mother, who stayed home to take care of Hillary and her brothers.

Hillary learned early in life to assert herself. A neighborhood family, the O'Callaghans, had a daughter named Suzy, who often bullied other children. Hillary was a small four-year-old when she became the frequent target of Suzy's fists. After being hit, Hillary would run home sobbing. One day her mother made an announcement. "There's no room in this house for cowards. You're going to have to stand up to her. The next time she hits you, I want you to hit her back."

Before long, Hillary faced Suzy again, and the confrontation soon attracted a circle of curious neighborhood kids. Nobody expected what happened next. Hillary—eyes closed—threw out her fist, knocking Suzy to the ground. The other children's mouths dropped open in awe. Hillary raced home, delighted with her triumph. She exclaimed to her mother that she was now tough enough to play with the boys.

The neighborhood in Park Ridge was full of families with young children. "There must have been forty or fifty children within a four-block radius of our house, and within four years of Hillary's age. They were all together, all the time, a big extended family . . . lots of playing and competition. She held her own at cops and robbers, hide and seek, chase and run," Hillary's mother recalled.

Hillary took piano lessons and ballet lessons. She played in a girls' softball league in summer and joined in pickup football and field hockey games with her brothers and other children. Ice-skating, swimming, and bike riding were other favorite activities. Hillary was a Brownie and then a Girl Scout. She took part in Scout parades, food drives, and cookie sales, and she earned almost every merit badge possible. At the age of nine, doctors found that Hillary was nearsighted, and she got her first pair of eyeglasses.

Seriously nearsighted, Hillary sometimes chose not to wear her thick eyeglasses because she didn't like how they looked. A friend would help her navigate through their neighborhood.

Along with friends, Hillary went to see movies at the Pickwick Theater. The whole family liked to go to Wrigley Field in Chicago to root for the Chicago Cubs baseball team. Every August they went to Hugh's father's cottage on Lake Winola in the Pocono Mountains of Pennsylvania.

## School of Hard Knocks

The Rodham family was financially secure. Hugh Rodham owned a successful business, and he always drove a Cadillac—a high-priced car. But the Rodham children were not pampered. Hugh routinely had the children rake leaves, cut the grass, pull weeds, and shovel snow. They all worked at his drapery shop when he needed extra help. He'd occasionally give the children some spending money but never a regular allowance. "They eat and sleep for free," he once grumbled. "We're not going to pay them for it as well!"

Hugh and Dorothy had grown up during the Great Depression (1929–1942), a period of economic hardship. Both their families had scraped and struggled to get by. Dorothy had had a particularly harsh childhood—she had been sent to live with her grandparents at the age of eight and was working full-time by the age of fourteen. As parents, Hugh and Dorothy wanted their children to appreciate their good fortune. On trips into downtown Chicago, they often drove through run-down neighborhoods so the children could see poverty up close.

Hillary felt sorry for children who weren't as well off as she was. When she was still in elementary school, she grew concerned about the children of Mexican migrant (traveling) workers, poor laborers who picked crops on farms near her home. Hillary decided to raise money and gather clothing for the workers' families. To raise funds, she organized carnivals and sports tournaments with neighborhood kids, charging a small fee to spectators. Later, she organized a babysitting service for the migrant children.

The biggest responsibility for the Rodham children was schoolwork. Hillary always earned top grades at school. At report card time,

**School days:** Hillary *(first row, far right)* with her sixth-grade classmates

Hillary remembers her mother praising her straight-A record. But her father made a snide remark. "You must go to a pretty easy school," he said when he saw her report card.

Early on, Hillary started thinking about a career. When she was fourteen, she wrote to the National Aeronautics and Space Administration (NASA). She was interested in the newly created space program, and she asked in her letter what she had to do to become an astronaut. An official at NASA soon answered. "We are not accepting girls as astronauts," he wrote. Hillary remembers being furious with this reply.

## Political Awakenings

Hillary was active at the First United Methodist Church, located in a redbrick building not far from the Rodham house. She attended Bible school, Sunday school, and a youth group there. When Hillary was in ninth grade, the Reverend Donald Jones arrived from New York City to become the church's new youth minister.

For several years, Hillary attended Jones's Methodist Youth Fellowship sessions. Jones called these classes the University of Life.

www.usatoday.com

**USA TODAY**

# News

SECTION A

## May 10, 2007

# The women of Mercury 13

<u>From the Pages of</u>
<u>USA TODAY</u>

Astronauts John Glenn and Alan Sheppard got the attention, but behind the scenes female pilots were also preparing for the rigors of space. Though they never got the call, these trailblazers laid the critical groundwork for those women who would reach the skies.

When 78-year-old Geraldine "Jerri" Sloan Trujillo learned that she and 12 other female pilots will get honorary doctor of science degrees from the University of Wisconsin-Oshkosh on Saturday, she was shocked. "Isn't that great?" she said in her thick Texas accent. "We're just used to rejection."

The "we" she was referring to are the Mercury 13, the highly accomplished female pilots who tried unsuccessfully to be accepted into NASA's astronaut corps in the early days of the space program. Few Americans know their names: Trujillo, Myrtle Cagle, Geraldine "Jerrie" Cobb, Jan Dietrich, Marion Dietrich, Mary Wallace "Wally" Funk, Jane Briggs Hart, Jean Hixson, Gene Nora Jesse, Irene Leverton, Sarah Pratley, Bernice "B" Steadman and Rhea Allison Wolman. But from 1960 to 1962, while the nation followed the exploits of John Glenn, Alan Sheppard and other Project Mercury astronauts, they secretly passed the same grueling medical tests.

President Johnson shut down the experiment, concluding that there was no need for women in space. Though barred from being military jet test pilots, many women racked up more flight hours than the male astronauts, and several outperformed the men on endurance tests. Two are now deceased, and three are too ill or have other commitments and won't attend the ceremony. Survivors range in age from 67 to 85.

—Sheryl McCarthy

All the teenagers in the youth group were white and middle class. Jones wanted them to learn about people from other backgrounds, so he took them to churches on Chicago's South Side. There, they met and talked with street kids, gang members, African Americans, and Hispanics.

In 1962 the group traveled to Orchestra Hall in Chicago to hear a speech by civil rights leader Martin Luther King Jr. King talked about racial injustice, poverty, and the struggle to end segregation (the separation of races) in the United States. After the speech, Jones took his group backstage and introduced the teenagers, including Hillary, to Dr. King. At the time, Hillary was only dimly aware of the civil rights movement and other protest movements taking place across the United States. King's words began to open her eyes to the national scene.

At high school—first Maine East High and later Maine South—Hillary earned high grades every year. She joined the National Honor Society and organized the junior prom. She also made her first venture into politics in those years. She successfully ran for student council and junior class vice president. She also served on a student group called the Cultural Values Committee, which tried to promote unity, respect, and understanding among students from different social backgrounds. During her senior year, she ran for student government president but lost the election.

Hillary was interested in national politics as well. Her father was a solid Republican, and at first, Hillary followed in his political footsteps. The Republican Party believed in free enterprise—the idea that private businesses should be able to operate with very little government interference. The Republicans didn't think government should try to solve social problems such as poverty or racial discrimination. In the 1950s and 1960s, the Republicans greatly distrusted the Communist Soviet Union (a union of fifteen republics including Russia) and worried about Communism spreading to many nations throughout the world.

Hillary thought the Republican ideas made sense. She joined a group called the Young Republicans and an anti-Communist club. During her senior year, in 1964, she campaigned for presidential candidate Barry Goldwater, a conservative Republican. As a "Goldwater girl," she wore a cowboy costume and a straw hat with the slogan "AuH$_2$O," which stood for "gold water."

The letters AuH$_2$0 come from chemistry's periodic table of the elements, which lists the chemical substances that make up all matter. *Au* stands for *aurum*, the Latin word for "gold." H$_2$0 is the chemical way to write water.

Her civics teacher, Jerry Baker, organized a mock presidential debate, with students playing the part of the two presidential candidates: Goldwater for the Republicans and President Lyndon Johnson for the Democrats. Baker wanted students to open their minds to opposing political viewpoints, so he had Ellen Press, a girl who normally backed the Democrats, play the part of Goldwater. He had Hillary, a Young Republican, play the part of Johnson. To prepare for the debate, Hillary recalls, "I immersed myself—for the first time—in President Johnson's Democratic positions on civil rights, health care, poverty, and foreign policy." As she became more and more familiar with the issues, she began to have a few doubts about her Republican leanings.

During her senior year, Hillary considered her options for college.

**School days:** Hillary *(standing)* poses with classmates in this 1964 yearbook photo.

# Communism

Hugh Rodham, along with many of his generation, thought Communists were a low form of life. Communists favor a state-run economy, with no private property or free enterprise. These restrictions angered a businessman like Hugh Rodham, and Hillary heard plenty along these lines as she was growing up.

When Hugh had fought in World War II, the Soviet Union, a Communist nation, was an ally. After the war, the differences between the U.S. capitalist system—which encourages privately owned property and businesses—and the Soviet Union's system put the two countries at odds. In fact, after the war, several nations near the Soviet Union became Communist too. The U.S. government worried that Communism was spreading. The fear was communicated to the U.S. public, which began to suspect that anyone who challenged the government's actions was a Communist.

Encouraged by two teachers, she applied to (and was accepted by) Smith and Wellesley, both women's colleges in Massachusetts. She never visited the campuses, but she talked to alumni and students and reviewed each school's promotional literature. She chose Wellesley, in part because the campus had a small lake, Lake Waban, that reminded her of Lake Winola in Pennsylvania.

Hillary graduated from high school with many honors, including a social science award. Of the 566 students in her class, she stood in the top 5 percent. In the fall of 1965, Hillary and her parents drove from Illinois to Massachusetts, where Hillary would begin her freshman year at Wellesley.

**Big changes:** Hillary arrived at Wellesley College in 1965. The prestigious school is selective in picking its students and is consistently in the top-five list of liberal arts colleges in the United States.

# An Explosion of Ideas

When Hillary Rodham arrived at Wellesley College, in the charming New England town of Wellesley, Massachusetts, she found herself at a school steeped in tradition. One of seven top-level women's colleges called the Seven Sisters, Wellesley had been founded in 1870. In 1965, when Rodham arrived, Wellesley students followed a strict code of conduct. They had to wear skirts to dinner. They had to obey a curfew (be in their dorm rooms by a certain hour). Young men weren't allowed to visit them in their rooms except on Sunday afternoons.

Almost all the Wellesley students were white. Some belonged to the nation's most prominent and wealthiest families. Rodham met young women who had graduated from private boarding schools, lived in Europe, and spoke foreign languages fluently. The only time Rodham had left the country was to see Niagara Falls in Canada. The school was "all very rich and fancy and very intimidating to my way of thinking," she remembers.

Rodham felt out of place at first, but she quickly adjusted to her new surroundings. She moved into Stone-Davis, a grand old dormitory on the shores of Lake Waban. She jumped into campus activities, joining the school's Young Republicans club and becoming its president. On weekends she dated young men, mostly students from nearby Harvard and other elite colleges. On Sundays she attended services at the local Methodist church.

## A New American Revolution

Hillary Rodham and her Wellesley classmates enjoyed a serene life on campus. But outside the sheltered college environment, the United States was undergoing big changes. In early 1965, Martin Luther King Jr. had led dramatic—but nonviolent—antisegregation marches in Alabama. Later that year, protesters had arrived in Washington, D.C., to speak out against U.S. involvement in the Vietnam War, which was raging in Southeast Asia. Groups such as Students for a Democratic Society began to question U.S. government policies regarding war, business, politics, and race relations. Women began to question their traditional, limited roles as mothers and housekeepers. Popular musicians—artists such as Bob Dylan and Joan Baez—sang about peace and justice.

A political and cultural revolution had started to sweep the nation, especially on college campuses. Soon even the well-brought-up, wealthy young women of Wellesley were talking about changing

# Young Republicans

The Young Republicans (YRs) is a grassroots U.S. political youth organization that contacts registered Republican voters who are eighteen to forty years old. Members supply voters with information from the Republican Party's point of view about candidates and the issues of the day.

First organized in New York City in 1859, YRs helped elect Abraham Lincoln in the 1860 presidential election. The group remained localized until the 1930s, when a West Point graduate named George H. Olmsted so impressed then president Herbert Hoover that he asked Olmsted to form a youth division of the Republican Party. Olmsted established the division, called the Young Republican National Federation (YRNF), and served as its first president.

The job of YRs is to recruit, train, and mobilize people to vote for Republican candidates and to participate in political campaigns. As such, the organization has been the proving ground for many members who later sought and won election to state and national public office, as well as members who became campaign consultants and community leaders.

society. Many abandoned their prim hairdos and nicely pressed outfits and adopted the newly fashionable "flower child" look, complete with bell-bottom blue jeans, headbands, peace symbols, and tie-dyed T-shirts.

Hillary Rodham began to read a magazine called *motive*. Published by the Methodist Church, the magazine examined the civil rights struggle, the Vietnam War, and other timely issues. She discussed and debated current affairs with her classmates and professors. She took courses in sociology, philosophy, and psychology. She eventually majored in political science. "My mind exploded when I got to Wellesley," Rodham remembered.

About a year after arriving at college, she abandoned the Republican beliefs she had once shared with her father. She no longer thought that government should ignore social issues and let big business operate as it pleased. She thought instead that government should help people—all people: black and white, young and old, rich and poor, male and female—to improve their own lives. She resigned from the Young Republicans.

Rodham began to learn everything she could about the Vietnam War (1957–1975). The United States had entered the war to help South Vietnam, which was fighting a takeover by Communist North Vietnam. Many students, including Hillary Rodham, thought the United States should withdraw from the war and let the Vietnamese people decide their own future. But the U.S. government was determined not to let South Vietnam fall to the Communists. The government sent thousands and thousands of soldiers to Vietnam. The more soldiers it sent, the more other young people in the United States protested against the war. Some young men who were drafted into (selected for) the military refused to fight.

During her junior year, in 1967, Rodham wanted to do her part to stop U.S. involvement in the Vietnam War. She joined the campaign of Eugene McCarthy—a Democrat and an antiwar senator from Minnesota. McCarthy was trying to win

**College girl:** Hillary became involved in many political causes while at Wellesley, including the presidential campaign of Democrat Eugene McCarthy.

the 1968 Democratic presidential nomination. On weekends, Rodham and a few friends would drive more than an hour to New Hampshire to stuff envelopes and do other work for the McCarthy campaign.

Early in 1968, Rodham engaged in yet another political campaign—her own race for student body president. After campaigning enthusiastically in the Wellesley dorms, she beat out two opponents for the job.

## Painful Lessons

The year 1968 was difficult for the United States. The Vietnam War continued to rage in Asia. Antiwar protests got larger and larger. The movement for civil rights became more vocal and sometimes violent. Then, on April 4, 1968, a gunman killed civil rights leader Dr. Martin Luther King Jr. in Memphis, Tennessee.

Since meeting Martin Luther King as a teenager, Rodham had spent many hours reading about King, his tactics of nonviolent protest, and his work to achieve equality for African Americans. She, like other Americans, was saddened by the assassination. Rodham joined a crowd in downtown Boston, Massachusetts, to peacefully protest the event and to mourn King's death.

Two months after King's assassination, Senator Robert F. Kennedy (seeking the Democratic presidential nomination) was shot and killed in Los Angeles, California. To compound the tragedy, Robert Kennedy was the brother of President John F. Kennedy, who had

### USA TODAY Snapshots®

A look at statistics that shape the nation

## Crimes of the century

Americans selected the assassination of John F. Kennedy as the worst high-profile crime in the USA this century. Their responses:

JFK assassination, 1963 — **36%**

Oklahoma City bombing, 1995 — **24%**

Martin Luther King assassination, 1968 — **11%**

O.J. Simpson case, 1994-95 — **10%**

Watergate break-in, 1972 — **5%**

Not — **14%**

Source: APBnews.com; Zogpy Poll    By James Abundis and Genevieve Lynn, USA TODAY, 2000

# IN FOCUS

## Martin Luther King Jr.

Born in Georgia in 1929, Martin Luther King Jr. grew up fast. He was in college by the age of fifteen and was an ordained minister at nineteen. By 1955 he'd earned his doctorate and was already at work in the growing civil rights movement. He gave stirring speeches in support of desegregation and supported nonviolent boycotts and sit-ins. He endured arrests, physical attacks, and police disrespect for his belief that all Americans deserved to enjoy civil rights.

By the early 1960s, he was well known as the leader of efforts to end segregation in all areas of public life—from transportation to voting to schooling—throughout the United States. His "I have a dream" speech at the Lincoln Memorial in 1963, wherein he painted a picture of a time when people would be judged by what they did with their lives and not how they looked, became an iconic moment in U.S. history.

In 1964 he won the Nobel Peace Prize for his nonviolent work and was on hand when President Lyndon Johnson signed into law the Civil Rights Act he and others had worked so hard to pass. Despite these strides, more progress was needed. He redoubled efforts to remove barriers for African Americans who wanted to vote and rejoiced when the Voting Rights Act became law.

By the late 1960s, frustration among some African Americans about the slow pace of change caused them to consider violence as an option. Dr. King had rejected this position all his life. He was assassinated in Memphis, Tennessee, in 1968, while trying to calm conflicts between striking workers, protesters, and the police.

been assassinated five years before. To many Americans, the United States seemed to be falling into chaos. The nation went into mourning once more.

Distressed about the killings but nevertheless hopeful, Hillary Rodham left Wellesley for a summer internship in Washington, D.C. The internship would give her firsthand experience with the workings of the U.S. government. But her plans had taken a strange twist. When she had arrived at Wellesley, she had been a Republican. So the professor in charge of the internship program scheduled her to intern for a group of Republican congresspeople. Rodham protested the assignment—after all, she had lately become a Democrat—but the job couldn't be changed.

Rodham knew she could learn plenty from the Republicans as well as the Democrats. In Washington that summer, she talked about the Vietnam War with members of Congress. She met important government officials, including Congressman Gerald Ford (later U.S. president). She even attended the Republican National Convention in Miami, Florida, where Richard Nixon won the presidential nomination.

When her internship ended in August, Rodham returned to Park Ridge to visit her family for a few weeks before returning to school. The Democrats were holding their presidential convention in downtown Chicago that summer. Thousands of demonstrators had gathered in nearby Grant Park to protest U.S. involvement in the Vietnam War. Rodham and a friend from high school, Betsy Johnson, wanted to witness the demonstration in person, so they took the train from Park Ridge to downtown Chicago.

They were not prepared for what they saw at the park. The protest had turned into a violent confrontation between demonstrators and the police. "You could smell the tear gas before you saw the lines of police," Rodham remembered. "In the crowd behind us, someone screamed profanities and threw a rock, which just missed us. Betsy and I scrambled to get away as the police charged the crowd with nightsticks."

Rodham was upset by the violence. She was convinced that rock throwing and tear gas would never solve political problems. The best ways to change government or society, she believed, involved nonviolent protest—like that used by Martin Luther King Jr.—as well as "working within the system." People who wanted change, she thought, needed to run for office, take jobs in law and government, and work peacefully within community organizations to achieve their goals. For her own part, Rodham wanted to work within the system by becoming a lawyer.

## August 21, 1996

# When conventional politics failed and idealism faded

<u>From the Pages of USA TODAY</u>   The return of the Democrats to the streets of Chicago is certain to touch off a media bout of nostalgia overload as every pundit and politico over the age of 40 will feel compelled to weigh in with their own personalized hot-time-in-the-old-town memories of billy clubs, tear gas and stink bombs.

While it is now fashionable to ridicule the self-indulgent excesses of the '60s, I prefer to recall those aspects of that turbulent decade that have been excised from our collective memory bank. What I remember is a naive yet intense idealism that wanted to remake America into a nation without racial divisions, without slums and festering inner cities, without insurmountable barriers between the rich and the poor and, yes, without an ugly and unnecessary war in Vietnam.

As television relives the cops-vs.-the-kids skirmishes in Chicago, it should be remembered, without excusing violence, that conventional politics failed in 1968. Martin Luther King Jr. and Robert Kennedy fell to assassins' bullets. Anti-war voters dominated the Democratic primaries, only to have old-time bosses hand the nomination to Hubert Humphrey. With the nation bitterly divided over Vietnam, the electorate was given an empty choice between Richard Nixon's war and the hapless Humphrey clinging to the bellicose but futile war policies of LBJ.

What saddens me is not only the tragic waste of Vietnam, but also the lost idealism of the 1960s. Among hawks who saw America locked in a worldwide struggle for freedom and doves who embraced a moral calling in stopping the napalm and the bombing, there was a shared belief that America was not just a country but a cause. Somehow we have lost that certainty of purpose in the aftermath of the Cold War. Instead of victory parades hailing the death of communism, we are mired in the petty politics of tax cuts and balanced budgets.

—Walter Shapiro, from the Opinion page

## Senioritis

By her senior year at Wellesley, Hillary Rodham was a confident young woman. She was a top student and student body president, with a long list of accomplishments to her name. So when she applied to law school at Yale and Harvard—the best programs in the nation—she was quickly accepted by both universities. When trying to choose between the two schools, Rodham met a Harvard professor. "We don't need any more women at Harvard," he coldly told her. That comment soured her on Harvard, so she chose Yale.

May 31, 1969, was graduation day for the Wellesley seniors. Their official commencement speaker would be Massachusetts senator Edward Brooke. But someone else was scheduled to speak as well: class president Hillary Rodham. In front of her father (her mother was home sick), teachers, and classmates, Rodham took her turn at the podium. The speech she made—written with the help of classmates—sharply criticized the administration of Richard Nixon, who had won

**Graduation day:** Hillary *(second from left)* gave a speech at her Wellesley commencement in May 1969.

the 1968 presidential election. She urged her fellow students to continue to protest against the government—but to do so constructively. Her words were hopeful and stirring.

> The question of possible and impossible was one that we brought with us to Wellesley four years ago. We arrived not yet knowing what was not possible. Consequently, we expected a lot. Our attitudes are easily understood having grown up ... [during] years dominated by men with dreams, men in the civil rights movement, the Peace Corps, the space program. . . . We found ... that there was a gap between expectation and realities. But it wasn't a discouraging gap and it didn't turn us into cynical, bitter old women at the age of 18. It just inspired us to do something about that gap.

To Rodham's surprise, the speech attracted attention nationwide. *Life* magazine published an article about her, along with her photograph. Reporters called her mother at home in Park Ridge. Many young people were speaking out at the time—criticizing the war, calling for women's rights, and fighting for social justice. But Hillary Rodham stood out from the crowd. In calling her fellow students to action, observers said, Hillary Rodham had spoken for an entire generation.

 Other Wellesley graduates include newscaster Diane Sawyer and former secretary of state Madeleine Albright.

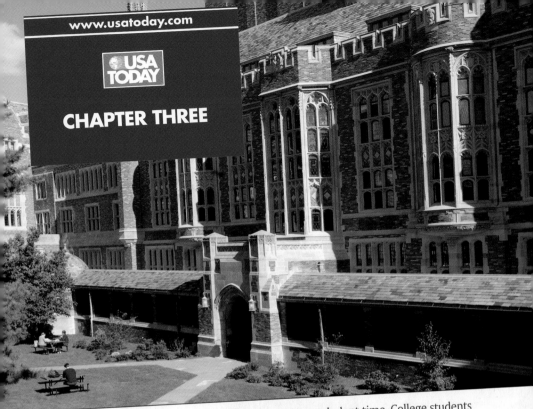

**Yale bound:** Hillary attended Yale Law School in a turbulent time. College students across the nation were trying to promote change in many ways, including participating in war protests and civil rights marches.

# From Yale to Arkansas

■■■■

Hillary Rodham entered Yale Law School in the fall of 1969. Like Wellesley, Yale was a school steeped in wealth and tradition. But the campus was alive with new ideas in 1969. Like college students around the country, Yale students were active in the civil rights movement, the antiwar movement, and the women's movement.

During her first year, 1969–1970, Rodham focused intently on her law school classes. But there were many distractions. Some of her classmates demonstrated in support of the Black Panthers, a radical African American political organization. Even more students demonstrated against the expansion of the Vietnam War from Vietnam into neighboring Cambodia. Rodham helped lead a large meeting, where Yale law students voted to take a stand against the war. But Rodham didn't agree with student protesters who used violence. She was determined to change society by working within the system.

Because of all the press attention from her Wellesley commencement speech, Rodham received many invitations to speak at political events. The League of Women Voters invited her to speak at a meeting on May 7, 1970. At the meeting in Washington, D.C., Rodham argued against the expansion of the Vietnam War. She also met the meeting's keynote speaker, Marian Wright Edelman, a civil rights advocate.

Edelman was starting an antipoverty organization in Washington, D.C., and Rodham asked for a summer job with the group. Rodham could have the job, Edelman replied, but the group had no money to pay her a salary. Undeterred, Rodham applied for and won a grant (an award of money) from a civil rights organization. The grant enabled her to live and work in Washington even without a salary.

Rodham's work that summer involved doing research on the education and health of the children of migrant farmworkers. This research focused her attention on the plight of children living in poverty. When she returned to Yale in the fall, she decided to make children's rights the focus of her law school studies.

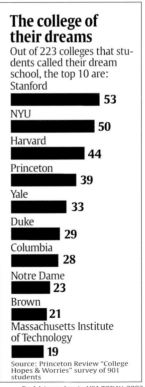

**The college of their dreams**

Out of 223 colleges that students called their dream school, the top 10 are:

Stanford **53**
NYU **50**
Harvard **44**
Princeton **39**
Yale **33**
Duke **29**
Columbia **28**
Notre Dame **23**
Brown **21**
Massachusetts Institute of Technology **19**

Source: Princeton Review "College Hopes & Worries" survey of 901 students

By Adrienne Lewis, USA TODAY, 2003

## A Handsome Stranger

In the fall of 1970, a young man arrived on the Yale campus. He had just returned from Oxford University in Great Britain, where he had been a Rhodes Scholar—winner of a prestigious academic award. He was a tall, charming Arkansan with a full beard and curly brown hair. He was William Jefferson Clinton, who went by the name of Bill.

Toward the end of the school year, in the spring of 1971, Bill Clinton was talking with a friend in the law school library when someone distracted him. A young woman wearing a flannel shirt and thick glasses was reading at the other end of the room. He couldn't stop staring at her. When she looked up from her book, she noticed him watching her, and she stared back. Finally, she shut her book, walked down to where Clinton sat, and said, "If you're going to keep looking at me, and I'm going to keep looking back, we might as well be introduced. I'm Hillary Rodham."

In fact, Hillary Rodham and Bill Clinton already knew about each other. She had seen him on campus and asked friends about him. She thought he was handsome and intriguing. He had seen her speak in class, and he knew about her news-making speech at the Wellesley commencement several years earlier. He thought she was magnetic and brilliant. He called her "the greatest thing on two legs."

**Yale couple:** Bill and Hillary became serious about each other while at Yale Law School.

Of Bill Clinton, Hillary later wrote, "No one understands me better and no one can make me laugh the way Bill does. . . . He is still the most interesting, energizing and fully alive person I have ever met."

Before long, the two were dating. But as the relationship turned more serious, both Rodham and Clinton wondered whether they could have a future together. She wanted to work as an attorney after law school, focusing on children's rights and other social causes, preferably in a big city. He had different goals altogether. "I'm going back to Arkansas, and I'm going to be governor," Clinton boldly told a lawyer who asked about his career plans. Of course, Clinton was just boasting. He knew he couldn't start his political career at the top of state government. But he was definitely set on holding political office.

During the summer and fall of 1972, Rodham and Clinton moved to Texas to work on the presidential campaign of Democratic senator George McGovern. Rodham worked in San Antonio, trying to register Hispanic voters. Clinton ran McGovern's state campaign headquarters in Austin. When the election arrived in November, McGovern made a poor showing. He was soundly defeated by his Republican opponent, President Richard Nixon.

Normally, law school at Yale lasts three years, but Rodham stayed for one extra year. She took a special course of study at the Yale Child Study Center. There, she took part in research on child development. At the same time, she helped several professors write a book on children and the law, she helped the Yale–New Haven Hospital draft guidelines for dealing with abused children, and she worked with foster children and foster parents at the New Haven Legal Services office.

Both Hillary Rodham and Bill Clinton finished their studies at Yale in the spring of 1973. Then they traveled to Britain, where they visited galleries, cathedrals, and historic ruins. On this trip, in the Lake District of northwestern England, Clinton asked Rodham to marry him. She loved him, but she wasn't sure about making a lifetime promise to him. She told him she wasn't ready for marriage.

## Career Paths

When the summer ended, Clinton and Rodham went separate ways. As planned, Clinton returned to Arkansas to prepare for a career in politics. He took a teaching job at the University of Arkansas Law School in Fayetteville, but he also began work on his first political campaign—a run for Congress. Rodham moved to Cambridge, Massachusetts. There, she took a job as a staff attorney for the Children's Defense Fund (CDF), a new organization created by Marian Wright Edelman. Although living more than 1,000 miles (1,600 kilometers) apart, Rodham and Clinton kept in frequent touch by letters and phone. He came to visit her at Thanksgiving, and she visited him at Christmas.

**Long-distance love:** Bill and Hillary moved to different cities and careers in 1973, but they kept up a relationship via letters, phone calls, and occasional visits.

# IN FOCUS

## The Children's Defense Fund

Founded by Marian Wright Edelman in 1973, the Children's Defense Fund (CDF) grew out of Edelman's work in the civil rights movement and in the Washington Research Project, which reviewed government programs for low-income families.

The CDF took this work a step farther and vocally advocated for programs—both private and government funded—that gave kids access to health care, proper nutrition, and education. The group researches and analyzes existing programs and reports to voters on how well their lawmakers are serving children. The CDF lobbies Congress for money and legislation that benefits children, particularly in the areas of education and health care. The group sparks grassroots efforts by organizing events, such as Stand for Healthy Children Day and Stand for Quality Child Care Day, as well as large rallies to mobilize voters and alert leaders in Washington, D.C., of CDF concerns. Through these efforts, the CDF has kept the needs of children in the national spotlight.

In late 1973, the House Judiciary Committee (part of the House of Representatives) was putting together a team to investigate President Nixon. In an incident called Watergate, Nixon and his staff were accused of trying to win the 1972 election by using burglary, wiretapping, and spying against their Democratic opponents, then covering up their crimes. The head of the investigation team asked a colleague to recommend some sharp young lawyers to join his staff. The colleague recommended Hillary Rodham and Bill Clinton, along with two other recent Yale Law School graduates.

The job would involve long hours, low pay, and a move to Washington, D.C. Clinton was busy with his run for Congress, so he turned down the offer. But Rodham was intrigued by the idea. Like other Americans, she was upset that the president was suspected of wrongdoing. She also knew that the Watergate investigation would be a historic case—no president

had ever been ac-
cused of such seri-
ous crimes before.
Rodham jumped
at the chance to be
part of history.

In January 1974,
Rodham joined
the Watergate in-
vestigation team.
The group's goal
was to gather evi-
dence that could
impeach Nixon—in
other words, charge
him with a serious

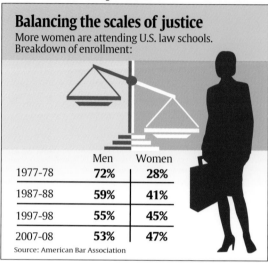

## USA TODAY Snapshots®

### Balancing the scales of justice

More women are attending U.S. law schools.
Breakdown of enrollment:

|  | Men | Women |
| --- | --- | --- |
| 1977-78 | 72% | 28% |
| 1987-88 | 59% | 41% |
| 1997-98 | 55% | 45% |
| 2007-08 | 53% | 47% |

Source: American Bar Association

By Anne R. Carey and Keith Simmons, USA TODAY, 2008

crime. But in August, before the full case could be brought against him, Nixon resigned from the presidency. He knew he would be found guilty, and he knew the American people had lost faith in him.

With Nixon's resignation, Rodham's job in Washington, D.C., ended. She sifted through job offers from law firms in Washington, New York, and Chicago. She was at a critical point in her career. Finally, she made a difficult decision—one that shocked and dismayed her friends. She decided to move to Fayetteville, Arkansas. She accepted a job teaching criminal law at the University of Arkansas Law School, the same school where Bill Clinton was teaching.

"Are you out of your mind," said Rodham's friend Sara Ehrman when she heard the news. "Why on earth would you throw away your future?" Arkansas was a poor, rural state with a total population of about one-quarter that of New York City. Why would Rodham want to live in sleepy Fayetteville when she could have her pick of high-paying, high-powered jobs in a big city? The answer was simple: Hillary Rodham loved Bill Clinton. She had decided to follow her heart to Arkansas.

## October 5, 1998

# Players in both inquiries

From the Pages of
USA TODAY

Wearing blue jeans and big granny glasses, she arrived on Capitol Hill in January 1974 as a wide-eyed, 26-year-old lawyer for the House Watergate hearings.

"I felt like I was walking around with my mouth open all the time," the Yale law school graduate told a biographer of those heady days working at the vortex of history.

Hillary Rodham was assigned to draft procedural rules for the Watergate proceedings. She recommended what kind of subpoena power [legal requirement to appear in court] would be enforced and what rules of evidence would apply. Other relatively junior people involved in Watergate have bloomed into major power players [in the Bill Clinton impeachment inquiry].

They include three members of the House Judiciary Committee of 1974: Rep. John Conyers, D-Mich., then 44 and a mid-level member, is now leading the panel's Democrats. A liberal, he pursued Nixon's impeachment. Senate Majority Leader Trent Lott, R-Miss., then a 32-year-old freshman member, was one of 10 committee Republicans who vot-

**Impeachment hearings:** Hillary *(center)* and other lawyers discuss bringing impeachment charges against President Richard Nixon in 1974.

ed against each of the three articles of impeachment against Nixon that passed. Defense Secretary William Cohen, then a 33-year-old moderate Republican, repeatedly sought bipartisan compromise on the panel. He voted for two of the three [Nixon] impeachment articles.

—Wendy Koch

**New home in Arkansas:** Hillary moved to Clinton's home state in 1974. She helped Bill with his campaign for Congress.

# First Lady of Arkansas

■■■■■

Fayetteville is a small college town in the Ozark Mountains. It has hilly, tree-lined streets and lovely Victorian houses. Hillary Rodham arrived in town in August 1974. She rented a three-bedroom house and jumped into her teaching job with her usual energy and commitment. By the fall of 1974, Bill Clinton's campaign for Congress was in full swing. During her spare time, Rodham helped at campaign headquarters. But when the election came in November, Clinton lost by a small margin.

As a law school professor, Rodham was demanding of and well respected by her students. In addition to teaching, she set up a university program to provide legal services for people in Fayetteville who could not afford lawyers. When the school year ended, Rodham took a summer trip to visit friends and family in Chicago, Boston, New York, and Washington, D.C. When she returned, Bill Clinton picked her up at the airport. But instead of taking her home, he drove up to a small redbrick house that she had admired earlier in the summer. He stopped the car. Much to Rodham's surprise, Clinton announced that he had bought the house, and he added: "Now you'd better marry me because I can't live in it by myself."

This time, she accepted his proposal. They didn't bother with a long engagement or elaborate wedding plans. They had a small wedding ceremony in the living room of the new house in October. Only close friends and family attended the ceremony. Then a larger group gathered in a friend's backyard for a reception. Nearly everyone had a

**Wedding bells:** Hillary and Bill married in their living room in October 1975 in Fayetteville, Arkansas.

good time at the party, but Bill Clinton's mother, Virginia Kelley, was upset. Before the wedding, Bill had told her that Hillary would not be taking the last name Clinton after she got married. She would keep the name Hillary Rodham. At the time, this was an unusual decision, and Clinton's traditional mother wasn't happy about it.

In another break with tradition, Bill and Hillary didn't take a typical honeymoon. Instead, they— along with Hillary's parents and Hillary's two brothers—took a vacation in Acapulco, Mexico, for ten days. "It was a honeymoon for six!" Hillary's brother Tony remarked.

## Picking up the Pace

The newlyweds' life in peaceful Fayetteville came to an end in late 1976, when Bill Clinton was elected to serve as Arkansas's attorney general—the state's chief law officer. This change required the couple to move to the Arkansas capital of Little Rock. Therefore, Rodham had to give up her teaching job in Fayetteville. Searching around for another position, she signed on with the Rose Law Firm, the most well-respected law practice in Arkansas.

She quickly became known as an energetic and determined lawyer. She worked on a variety of cases, including many involving the protection of children. Bill Clinton, meanwhile, was moving up fast. A popular attorney general, he decided the time was right to make a run for governor of Arkansas. He hit the campaign trail in early 1978. Attractive and well spoken, with a magnetic personality, he easily beat out four other candidates to win the Democratic primary (the race for the Democratic nomination). When the election rolled around in November, he easily won that too.

**First couple of Arkansas:** Hillary stands with her husband as he takes the oath of office as governor of Arkansas in 1978.

Only thirty-two years old and the youngest governor in the nation, Bill Clinton was nicknamed the boy governor. He and Rodham moved into the enormous Arkansas Governor's Mansion in Little Rock, complete with a cook and other staff members. Rodham continued working at the Rose Law Firm, which made her a partner (part owner) shortly after the election. As a partner, she earned far more money than her husband did as governor. She was just thirty-one. Neither could believe that they had come so far so fast.

When Bill was governor of Arkansas, Hillary earned more money as a lawyer than he did as the governor. Her salary was around one hundred thousand dollars. His was thirty-five thousand dollars.

## Arkansas Backlash

Many older, more traditional Arkansas citizens did not like the new governor or his wife, however. Although Bill Clinton was an Arkansas native, some people considered him an outsider. He had attended high-tone colleges on the East Coast, and many of his staff members were easterners. He had liberal views on social issues, such as women's rights. Some people called him a "long-haired hippie."

But critics saved their worst remarks for Hillary Rodham. Rodham had never paid much attention to fashion. Although she dressed in business attire on the job, she felt most comfortable in big sweaters and blue jeans. She wore thick, oversized glasses and refused to wear makeup. She had long, straight hair, which she rarely curled or styled. To many Arkansans, Rodham did not look like a proper state First Lady. They wanted a First Lady who wore a fashionable hairdo, cute outfits, jewelry, and lots of makeup. To make matters worse, Rodham was a Yankee, or northerner—an outsider who did not, many felt, understand or fit into Arkansas's southern culture. She was also an outspoken and ambitious businesswoman. That didn't sit right with some Arkansans either. They thought the governor's wife should be a prim and proper housewife.

While she was working hard as a lawyer and trying to adjust to her new role as First Lady, Rodham became pregnant. On February 17, 1980, she gave birth to a baby girl, Chelsea, named after a Joni Mitchell song, "Chelsea Morning." Chelsea was born a few weeks early, but she was healthy and weighed slightly over 6 pounds (3 kilograms). The Clintons were thrilled with their new baby. However, when newspapers reported that "Governor Bill Clinton and Hillary Rodham had a daughter," many citizens were offended. The majority of Arkansans thought the announcement should have read "Governor and Mrs. Bill Clinton."

Bill Clinton made some important strides for Arkansas during his term in office, including—with the help of his wife—reforming the state's health-care system. But some voters were still unhappy with his personal and political views. In 1980 Bill Clinton lost his bid for reelection. He was disappointed and depressed.

## A Comeback

The family left the Governor's Mansion and bought an old home in Little Rock. With the help of babysitters and nannies for Chelsea, Rodham and Clinton juggled work and parenthood. Bill Clinton took a job with a Little Rock law firm, but he was determined to win back the governor's job.

Rodham wanted to help her husband win any way she could, and she knew she might have to make some compromises to do so. So in early 1982, when Clinton announced that he was again running for governor, Rodham tried to give voters the image they wanted in a First Lady. For starters, she began calling herself Hillary Rodham Clinton. She also livened up her appearance with a new hairstyle with blonde streaks, contact lenses instead of glasses, lipstick and eye shadow, and a fashionable wardrobe.

Together the Clintons began to campaign nonstop. Hillary sat in on planning sessions and supported and encouraged her husband when he grew disheartened or tired. And she did a great job of convincing voters to accept his ideas and plans for the government.

The campaign was a success, and Bill won reelection in late 1982. Right away, he appointed Hillary as chairperson of the state's new Arkansas Education Standards Committee. The committee's job was to set standards for the quality of education throughout the state. Hillary traveled all over Arkansas to hold hearings and meet with groups of parents and teachers. In the end, the committee recommended some important changes, including required tests for teachers to prove their ability to teach.

More popular than he had been during his first term, Bill Clinton won reelection again in 1984 and 1986. Hillary remained involved in state programs. In 1985 she established the Home Instruction Program for Preschool Youth (HIPPY), which taught low-income Arkansas parents how to prepare their children for kindergarten. All the while, she practiced law, raised Chelsea, and continued her work on behalf of children. She served on the board of directors of several educational

**Many roles:** Hillary was busy in the 1980s, being a mom to Chelsea *(above)*, working at the Rose Law Firm, and serving on boards and organizations for different social justice and children's causes. She also had many duties as First Lady of Arkansas.

and social justice organizations, including the Children's Defense Fund. She also performed the jobs expected of a governor's wife, such as hosting teas and attending luncheons.

The family traveled and enjoyed their time together. But Hillary also had some worries. First and foremost, Bill Clinton had a reputation as a womanizer—a man who flirted, chased women, and cheated on his wife. On and off, rumors surfaced that Governor Clinton was having affairs with other women. The rumors hurt Hillary, but Bill assured her that they were untrue.

## Taking the Leap

In 1987 Bill Clinton was forty years old. His popularity and successes in Arkansas were well known. Many Democratic leaders began encouraging him to run for president of the United States. He and Hillary discussed the idea carefully, but they decided it was too soon. They knew his opponents would stir up bad press about his rumored

**August 8, 1988**

## First lady, lawyer

From the Pages of USA TODAY Hillary Clinton of Little Rock has a lot to say about the problems female lawyers face.

She spoke on the subject to the American Bar Association in Toronto Sunday. Issues include bias by judges and in law schools, as well as the intense competition within law firms that makes it hard to juggle 80-hour workweeks with family life. "The tradition-bound legal profession may have to change drastically to accommodate family needs," she says. Clinton, 40, is one of three female partners in the sixty-lawyer Rose law firm of Little Rock.

Besides her practice and duties as the state's first lady, Clinton has an 8-year-old daughter, but readily admits her situation is not typical of female lawyers: "There's a staff that runs and maintains the governor's mansion."

—Tony Mauro

---

affairs with other women. They thought Chelsea was too young to be exposed to the difficulties and possible ugliness of such a campaign. However, he was invited to give the nominating speech at the Democratic National Convention.

But four years later, after another two terms as governor, Bill Clinton was ready to step up to the next level. By then even more Democrats were encouraging Clinton to run for president. Finally, one morning in August 1991, Hillary woke up and peered into her husband's sleepy face. "You almost have to do it," she said—meaning run for president.

"Do you have any idea what we're getting into?" he asked. "I know, it'll be tough," she answered. But they were both ready for the challenge of a lifetime.

## CHAPTER FIVE

**Presidential run:** Bill, Chelsea, and Hillary have a family moment at the press conference in 1991 where Clinton announced his campaign for president of the United States.

# "The Race Is On"

On October 3, 1991, Bill Clinton stood in front of the Old State House in Little Rock and announced his intention to run for president of the United States. Amid a sea of microphones and TV cameras, he spoke passionately about the problems facing the nation: "Middle-class people are spending more time on the job, less time with their children and bringing home less money to pay more for health care and housing and education," he said. "The poverty rates are up, the streets are meaner and ever more children are growing up in broken families. Our country is headed in the wrong direction, fast." Clinton promised a new vision for the United States. He said that as president, he would bring more job opportunities, a better economy, and better schools and health-care services to Americans.

As usual, Hillary stood by his side as he spoke, as did Chelsea. The speech kicked off a whirlwind campaign that lasted more than a year

**www.usatoday.com**

**USA TODAY**

# News

### SECTION A

## October 4, 1991

# Clinton joins the '92 pack

### From the Pages of USA TODAY

With an appeal to the "forgotten middle class," Arkansas Gov. Bill Clinton began his presidential campaign Thursday. His platform is detailed, from college scholarships to health care, and is aimed at voters who have deserted the Democratic Party.

Clinton, 45, brought to the presidential stage his long-standing effort to move the party to the center and recapture once-loyal Democrats. He offered a blend of middle class-oriented programs, populist attacks on Wall Street, and a call on social service recipients to take "personal responsibility" in exchange for help.

Clinton, who had urged avoiding attacks on President Bush, assailed the GOP [Republican Party]:

"Everything we believe in, everything we've fought for, is threatened by an administration that turns its back on the middle class," he said. He vowed to "put government back on the side of the hard-working, middle-class families who think most help goes to the top of the ladder, some goes to the bottom, and nobody stands up for them. This has to be a campaign about ideas, not slogans," he said. Voters "already know what we're against. Let's show them what we're for."

—Adam Nagourney

and took the Clintons to every corner of the nation. As in earlier elections, Hillary was an integral part of her husband's campaign team. She helped Bill write speeches and took part in planning sessions.

Campaigning in New Hampshire one day, Clinton talked to supporters about his wife's extensive experience working on behalf of children and the poor. He explained that if he were elected, his wife would be an active partner in

**On the trail:** Hillary campaigned all over the country for her husband in 1992.

his new administration. He joked that "Buy one, get one free," should be his new campaign slogan.

Not everyone thought the joke was funny. Just like the voters in Arkansas, Americans in other places had a distinct image of how a national First Lady should act. They thought she should be quiet and ladylike, attending to social matters but in no way involved in running the government. Former president Richard Nixon summed up the feelings of many Americans when he commented about the Clintons, "If the wife comes through as being too strong and too intelligent, it makes the husband look like a wimp."

Hillary took a leave of absence from the Rose Law Firm to work on Bill's campaign full-time.

## "Stand by Your Man"

The Clintons were no strangers to criticism. And after Bill's twelve years as governor, they were no strangers to mean-spirited political campaigns. So they shrugged off the negative comments and continued their campaign travels.

But the attacks got even harsher. Like all political candidates, the Clintons were put under the microscope. The press combed through every detail of their personal lives, hounding their family members for childhood stories and photos and needling their friends for juicy tidbits about them. Not surprisingly, it wasn't long before rumors of Bill's extramarital affairs came to light in the media. According to one gossip magazine, a woman named Gennifer Flowers claimed to have had a twelve-year affair with Bill Clinton. Soon the story was all over television and the newspapers.

The story threatened to overshadow Bill Clinton's message about important issues facing the country. To put the rumors to rest, his campaign team decided that he and Hillary should go on TV's *60 Minutes* news show to set the record straight. The show aired right after the Super Bowl, on January 26, 1992, so a large audience was watching. During the interview, Bill denied having an extramarital affair with Gennifer Flowers. He added that he and Hillary loved each other very much but like all couples had had some difficult moments in their marriage.

Then Hillary added a comment of her own: "You know, I'm not sitting here, some little woman standing by my man like Tammy Wynette. I'm sitting here because I love him and I respect him and I honor what he's been through and what we've been through together. And you know, if that's not enough for people, then heck, don't vote for him."

Hillary was referring to Tammy Wynette's famous country song "Stand by Your Man." The song tells women to stick by their husbands through thick and thin, to love them without question, and to forgive them when they stray. Hillary's reference to the song stirred up more controversy. By belittling the lyrics, some people thought she was attacking traditional marriage and motherhood.

It seemed that Hillary's words were constantly being twisted, and offhand remarks kept coming back to haunt her. Another misunderstanding took place in Chicago in March, when a reporter asked her about charges of questionable dealings between the Rose Law Firm and the Arkansas state government. In explaining the situation, Hillary said: "You know, I suppose I could have stayed home and baked

**Meeting voters:** Hillary shakes hands with a man in New York City. She was campaigning for Bill before the state's primary election in 1992.

cookies and had teas, but what I decided to do was fulfill my profession, which I entered before my husband was in public life."

Hillary went on to say that she supported whatever a woman chose to do—whether that was working full-time, staying home with her kids, or doing some combination of both. But only the "cookies" comment made the evening news. Again, it seemed as if Hillary was putting down homemakers.

To be sure, Hillary Clinton was a proud feminist—someone who believes in complete equality between men and women. Some American voters—especially young women and working women—loved her bold statements, strong opinions, and professional achievements. But other, more traditional voters were put off by a woman who was ambitious and independent.

## July 16, 1992

# Hillary Clinton's image undergoes a change

<u>From the Pages of</u>
<u>USA TODAY</u>

The pastel suits have become a staple. The adoring gaze appears perfected. The vague talks about issues and plugs for chocolate-chip cookies are by rote.

Hillary Clinton came to New York to redefine her image as a supportive wife to presidential candidate Bill Clinton—a concession, it seemed, to an outcry among some voters. But as hundreds of women's rights activists and dozens of women candidates here lobby for power and clout, some are left wondering whether the outspoken Hillary Clinton they knew and loved several months ago is gone for good.

"It's a sad double-standard that we have when we look at the spouses of presidential candidates and expect them to somehow be different than female candidates," says Kitty Dukakis, wife of 1988 Democratic presidential nominee Michael Dukakis.

Eleanor Smeal of the Fund for the Feminist Majority says the Clinton campaign is making "a mistake" by remaking Hillary Clinton. Clinton "is educated and knows issues and is serious," Smeal says. "And we need serious leadership from women."

Hillary Clinton says that she hasn't changed at all in response to criticism of her outspokenness early in the campaign. A lawyer, lobbyist and corporate board member, she says she's always acted as a surrogate for her husband. But both liberal and conservative observers say the change is pronounced. "They have retrained her," says Beverly LaHaye of the conservative group Concerned Women for America. "It's a very wise political move because the way she really is . . . is very unappealing to voters."

But Ellen Malcolm of EMILY's List, a group that raises money for Democratic female candidates, says there are many sides to Hillary Clinton. "The real Hillary Clinton is a woman who has supported her husband's career and raised a family and had her own career," Malcolm says. At the same time, she says, the would-be first lady should speak out forcefully on the issues because she "is a wonderful role model fo' women."

—Mim'

**Official nomination:** The Clintons attend the Democratic National Convention in July 1992.

## The Home Stretch

Bill Clinton had his backers and his attackers too. During the primary race, he spoke in favor of abortion rights, gun control, and social programs. His liberal stances angered many conservative Americans. The press reported that during the Vietnam War, Bill Clinton, like many young men of the era, had tried to avoid military service. Many traditional Americans said he was unpatriotic.

But even with these criticisms, Bill Clinton's popularity soared. In July 1992, at the Democratic National Convention, he officially became his party's candidate for president. He would square off against President George H. W. Bush, the Republican candidate, and H. Ross Perot, an independent (a candidate not affiliated with any party).

Through the rest of the summer and into the fall, Bill and Hillary traveled by bus, together with vice-presidential candidate Al Gore and his wife, Tipper. They traveled thousands of miles, making speeches and boosting their support among voters. Hillary and Tipper became close friends during the journey.

The Clintons returned home to Little Rock on the morning of election day, November 3, 1992. They voted and then rested—but only briefly. Bill and Chelsea went for a jog together during the afternoon, and he later dropped into a neighborhood McDonald's for a soft drink and conversation with other customers. During the long evening, the family gathered with friends at the Arkansas Governor's Mansion and watched the election results on television. Bill Clinton was winning state after state.

Around ten that evening, President Bush conceded defeat. Bill Clinton would be the next president of the United States. Outside the Old Statehouse in Little Rock, crowds began to celebrate. Along with the Gores, the Clintons arrived onstage and waved to thousands of spectators and reporters. Bill gave a brief acceptance speech, and then the celebration continued. The long, hard race was over. The next stop was the White House, the president's home in Washington, D.C.

 After his victory, Bill and Hillary danced together to the old rock tune that had become the campaign's official song, Fleetwood Mac's "Don't Stop (Thinking about Tomorrow)."

**Power couples:** *(Left to right)* Hillary, Tipper Gore, Bill, and Al Gore celebrate their victory on election night 1992 in Little Rock, Arkansas.

**USA TODAY**

## CHAPTER SIX

**Presidential pose:** Bill was sworn into the office of president of the United States on January 21, 1993. Hillary held the Bible as her husband was sworn in. Chelsea is at left.

# Woman in the West Wing

On January 21, 1993, William Jefferson Clinton was sworn in as the forty-second president of the United States. Of course, the day represented a huge milestone for Bill. But Hillary and Chelsea, too, were faced with big changes. The whole family, along with their cat, Socks, moved to the White House at 1600 Pennsylvania Avenue in Washington, D.C. For Hillary, moving to Washington meant giving up her job at the Rose Law Firm and stepping into the role of First Lady. For Chelsea the move to Washington meant a new school and new friends and living in the bright spotlight as the daughter of the president of the United States.

Because Bill was a longtime governor, the family had been well known in Arkansas. They were used to se-

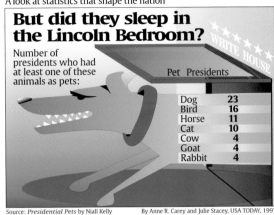

## USA TODAY Snapshots®
A look at statistics that shape the nation

### But did they sleep in the Lincoln Bedroom?

Number of presidents who had at least one of these animals as pets:

Pet Presidents

| Pet | Presidents |
|-----|------------|
| Dog | 23 |
| Bird | 16 |
| Horse | 11 |
| Cat | 10 |
| Cow | 4 |
| Goat | 4 |
| Rabbit | 4 |

Source: *Presidential Pets* by Niall Kelly     By Anne R. Carey and Julie Stacey, USA TODAY, 1997

curity guards and swarms of reporters. But as the First Family, their fame was far greater. Bill, Hillary, and Chelsea each had a team of Secret Service agents assigned to protect them around the clock. If Hillary wanted to take a quiet walk or bike ride, not only would several agents have to accompany her, but others would follow behind in a van.

The Secret Service gives code names to the president and his family members. Hillary's name was Evergreen. Bill's was Eagle, and Chelsea's was Energy.

Thirteen-year-old Chelsea enrolled in Sidwell Friends School, a small private school in Washington, D.C. Bill and Hillary had always promoted public education, so the decision to enroll their daughter in a private school caused a stir in the press. But Bill and Hillary were most concerned with shielding Chelsea's privacy. Private schools were off-limits to TV and newspaper reporters, whereas public schools were not. At Sidwell Friends, reporters could not bother Chelsea.

### First Lady of Health Care

Bill Clinton had discussed many pressing issues when he ran for president. He often spoke about problems with the nation's health-care system. Health insurance was so expensive that millions of people couldn't afford it, he explained. Many people got sick and even died because they couldn't pay to see a doctor. He promised that if he were elected president, he would reform the insurance industry and the health-care system in the United States.

Clinton knew the perfect person to handle such an important job—a person with years of experience working on behalf of families, children, working people, and the poor—a person who had successfully reformed the educational system in Arkansas. That person was his wife, Hillary Rodham Clinton. On January 25, less than a week after his inauguration, President Clinton appointed Hillary to head his Task Force on National Health Care Reform.

**Presidential appointment:** Hillary talks to reporters on Capitol Hill in Washington, D.C., along with Senator Bob Dole of Kansas, in April 1993. Hillary met with lawmakers to discuss health-care reform.

www.usatoday.com

**USA TODAY**

# News

SECTION A

**March 22, 1993**

# Hillary a role model for girls

<u>From the Pages of</u>
<u>USA TODAY</u>

My 10-year-old sister told me she wants to be like Hillary Clinton when she grows up. Hillary Rodham Clinton surfaced in "the year of the woman," and she is not only independent, successful, intelligent and able to balance family and career, she is visibly happy in her position and success, a rare combination. But my sister's admiration goes beyond the glamour of the White House. She associates the White House with success, intelligence and power for women. In Hillary Clinton's confident laugh and solid speeches, she detects the message, "I am proud to be a woman, and so should you be, too."

Hillary Clinton has already had a great influence on the youngest generation of females. Little girls, who look up to the first lady, raise their hands even higher, look into people's eyes when they speak and have high hopes for their own futures. My little sister wants to be a doctor, a writer, a disc jockey and have a family as well. She says that if the first lady can have a great career and a great family, so can she. The first lady has sent her the message that if she works hard and fights hard, she can be whatever she wants.

I wish I'd had a similar role model when I was 10. Perhaps just knowing that a woman could be so powerful and intelligent would have given me higher expectations of myself and my future. But it's not too late. Now, Hillary Clinton is my role model as well. Whenever I am facing a great challenge, I look at her face that glows with spunk and confidence and say, "I can be that as well."

This first lady has more than the responsibilities of presidential spouse. She's a role model to millions of girls and young women; and as my sister already discovered, Hillary Clinton is one tough act to follow.

—Amy Wu, from the Opinion page

No one was surprised to learn that Hillary Clinton would devote herself to an important cause. After all, several earlier First Ladies had worked on social issues. Eleanor Roosevelt, the wife of President Franklin D. Roosevelt, had worked tirelessly on behalf of minorities and the poor. President Lyndon Johnson's wife, Lady Bird, had devoted herself to beautifying the nation's highways and cities. Nancy Reagan, the wife of President Ronald Reagan, had spoken out against illegal drug use. But what was surprising was the nature of Hillary Clinton's assignment. No other First Lady had held an official job making government policy.

In addition to heading the health-care task force (she was not paid for the job), Hillary had a number of other jobs as First Lady. In keeping with tradition, she was the official White House hostess, in charge of overseeing dinners and receptions. She also had to make speeches, attend conferences, welcome foreign leaders, and visit foreign countries. She had a staff of twenty, including speechwriters, research assistants, travel directors, social directors, and secretaries.

Hillary set up her office in the West Wing of the White House. This was another break with tradition. First Ladies had always made their offices in the East Wing, not the West Wing, where the president and his senior advisers worked. But Hillary wanted her staff to be integrated with the rest of the White House staff. Their work on health care and other issues was just as important as everyone else's, she believed.

## Rough Waters

After all the earlier criticism, it wasn't surprising that many people also criticized Hillary for leading the task force on health care. They accused her of trying to grab too much power. Once when she was speaking in Lincoln, Nebraska, in April 1993, a woman held up a sign reading, "Hillary, Who Elected You President?" Other people posted signs that said "Impeach Hillary," implying that she, not her husband, was running the country. People also made jokes about "President Clinton and her husband, Bill."

## November 30, 1992

# Today's debate: Hillary Clinton and the role she should fill as first lady

<u>From the Pages of USA TODAY</u>

**OPPOSING VIEW: Hillary is qualified for any high-level position. Repeal the law that keeps her from serving.**

It is time to stop thinking about first ladies and recognize the first woman. Hillary is a role model for contemporary women and for millions of girls who aspire to achieve on equal footing with their brothers. To prevent a talented individual from serving the American people because she is married to the president is not fair to her or the nation. If Hillary had been elected president, no one would expect Bill to fill a token job, bake cookies or serve tea. Hillary is unquestionably qualified for a high-level appointment. President Clinton has said that this country cannot afford to lose the talents of a single individual. To sacrifice the abilities of Hillary to a bad law would be a deplorable waste.

—Martha Burk, president of the
Center for Advancement of Public Policy in Washington, D.C.

**OUR VIEW: Hillary Clinton doesn't need to head a federal agency to serve the nation.**

For the first time, a career woman who out earned her husband will become first lady. Despite clearly being qualified as a lawyer, child advocate and education reformer, she is rightly barred by federal law from serving as a member of the Cabinet or other appointed position under President Clinton's jurisdiction.

Equally wisely, Clinton has said he has no plans to make an issue of the law. Why should he? Appointed or not, Hillary Clinton already is one of the president's closest advisers.

She's a policy pro and trusted partner who can have more impact than noted first ladies of the past. A Cabinet job or other top-level position would offer only trouble. It would raise questions of favoritism and erode public support. Hillary's exceptional talents mean she'll make her presence felt without an exception to the law being made for her.

—*USA TODAY*'s editors

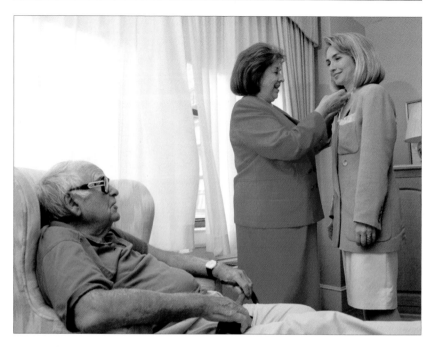

**Parental moment:** Hillary visits with her parents. Hugh Rodham died after suffering a stroke in 1993.

Hillary was tough. She took the criticism in stride and continued her work on health care and other issues. But on both a personal and a professional level, the family faced one difficulty after another. First, on March 19, 1993, Hillary's father suffered a massive stroke. The family flew to Little Rock to be by his bedside. He died less than three weeks later.

After a period of mourning, Bill and Hillary got back to work. But it seemed like bad news just kept coming. In May financial auditors found evidence of mismanagement in the White House Travel Office. It was a small matter, but critics of the Clintons blew it out of proportion, calling it Travelgate—a nickname that echoed the Watergate scandal of twenty years before.

A few months later, Deputy White House Counsel Vince Foster, an old friend of Hillary's from the Rose Law Firm, was found dead in a park outside Washington, D.C. He appeared to have committed suicide. But rumors swirled that his death was a murder and was somehow related to Travelgate—or perhaps to more sinister dealings within the Clinton administration.

One of the few bright spots came in September and October, when Hillary and Bill introduced their health-care reform legislation (a group of laws) to Congress. Along with other changes, the proposed plan included affordable health insurance for every American. Hillary was just the third First Lady to ever testify before Congress and the first to introduce major legislation. Those who heard her speak were impressed by her command of the complex health-care issue. Both Democrats and Republicans applauded her testimony and praised her recommendations for change. The lawmaking process is often slow, and the proposed reforms still had a long way to go before they would become law, but both Hillary and Bill were encouraged by the response.

**Testifying on reform:** Hillary speaks about health care at a committee hearing in the House of Representatives in 1993.

**September 28, 1993**

# First lady takes role as saleswoman

From the Pages of
USA TODAY

Although she never would say so, Hillary Rodham Clinton's public emergence today—at televised hearings on Capitol Hill—is a proclamation of power: The Clinton health-reform plan is her plan. And as she looks up this morning from her place at the witness table to the 36 somber-suited men and two women on the House Ways and Means Committee, she tacitly will defy all the critics who said months ago that a first lady never should be asked by her husband to create a major policy initiative, let alone be put in the position of defending one. But these days, it's hard to find anyone willing to say they find menace in her role. Even critics of the health plan say she's the right emissary—but for the wrong program. "Everyone will be very impressed with how smart she is and how much she knows," says conservative Rep. Newt Gingrich, R-Ga. "Then, they'll look at the plan."

As chief saleswoman of the president's American Health Security Act, Hillary Clinton probably won't be ambushed over the plan's financing or its coverage of abortions. But the signal is clear: This president trusts his wife to lead the crusade on which he has staked his presidency. So far, the public seems to agree. A new USA TODAY/CNN/Gallup Poll shows 60% approve of the way the first lady is handling health-care policy—up from 50% two weeks ago.

But Clinton's high-publicity role has more to do with getting the plan passed than acknowledging the first lady's clout: The White House is betting lawmakers' respect for her—nurtured in 130 private meetings—will make them conciliatory. In those private sessions, Clinton apparently charmed most she came into contact with, and muted a lot of opposition.

"She's a person of considerable substance," adds Sen. John Chafee, R-R.I. There are "some differences in the approach of the Republican senators and the administration's plan, but when we get into those, she is able to defend her position."

—Judy Keen and Mimi Hall

December 1993 was another dark period. It began when federal investigators accused the Whitewater Development Company, a corporation in Arkansas, of financial wrongdoing. The Clintons had been partners in the corporation when they lived in Arkansas. They denied they had ever acted illegally, but to clear the air, President Clinton promised to have the matter investigated.

About the same time the Whitewater charges hit the papers, more accusations came to light about Bill Clinton's womanizing during his days as Arkansas governor. The new stories, nicknamed Troopergate because they originated with Arkansas state troopers, were untrue. Bill and Hillary suspected that their political enemies had paid the troopers to make the accusations.

The next year, 1994, was hardly any better. In January Bill Clinton's mother, Virginia Kelley, died of breast cancer. Then Paula Jones, a former Arkansas state employee, accused Bill Clinton of sexual harassment (unwelcome sexual advances). Then an independent counsel (lawyer), appointed by federal judges, began investigating the Whitewater affair.

Finally, perhaps most disappointing of all for Hillary, her health-care plan "died" in Congress (was dropped from

**Another loss:** Bill's mother, Virginia Kelley *(right)*, died of breast cancer in 1994.

consideration) without ever coming to a vote. Millions of Americans supported her ideas for affordable health care. But insurance companies, drug companies, and other powerful groups had lobbied hard to discredit the plan, worried that it would cut into their profits.

By late 1994, Bill Clinton was finishing his second year as president. It seemed as if his Republican opponents had spent the previous two or three years doing nothing but attacking his wife, searching for scandals in his personal and business affairs, criticizing his policies, and investigating him. With all the negative press, voters seemed wary of Bill Clinton's Democratic administration. They expressed their displeasure by voting in a majority of Republican congresspeople and senators at the midterm elections in November.

# IN F⊙CUS

## U.S. Political Parties

Throughout much of the twentieth century and into the twenty-first century, Democrats and Republicans have tended to take opposing views on many issues. Democrats tend to view government as a tool for helping people improve their lives. They generally support the interests of poor and working people over the interests of big business, a view sometimes called liberal, or left wing. Republicans, sometimes called conservative, or right wing, usually prefer that government not try to solve social problems. They support policies that allow businesses to operate freely, without many government controls.

Labels such as liberal and conservative can be misleading and inaccurate, however. Many people have conservative views on some issues and liberal views on others. Many wealthy businesspeople support the Democrats, traditionally the party of poor people, and many working-class people support the Republicans, traditionally the party of the rich.

## Rebound

Was Bill Clinton doing a bad job as president? With all the scandals and accusations, it might seem so. But in fact, the opposite was true. Under Bill Clinton's watch, the U.S. economy was booming and unemployment was falling. The national debt—the vast sums of money the United States owed to other nations—was falling too. Inflation (rising prices) was low. Although he often had to fight with Republicans in Congress, especially Georgia congressman Newt Gingrich, Clinton was able to pass a number of important laws, such as gun control bills, environmental protection laws, and a minimum wage increase.

As for Hillary, she began to keep a lower profile after the defeat of her health-care plan. She no longer tried to promote major policy reforms. Instead, she traveled and met with foreign leaders, attended conferences, wrote articles, and made speeches. She continued to work on the issues that had always interested her: children's rights, women's rights, education, and improving life for the poor.

As one of the most famous women on the planet, Hillary met with people around the world, who were eager to hear her speak. She and Chelsea traveled to India, Pakistan, Nepal, Sri Lanka, and Bangladesh, focusing their attention on improving women's rights and children's rights in those countries. She welcomed the opportunity to discuss causes in which she so strongly believed.

**Traveling team:** Hillary and Chelsea visit an orphanage in India on one of their trips abroad in 1995.

In 1995 Hillary spoke forcefully at the United Nations' Fourth World Conference on Women in Beijing, China. She identified the abuses faced by women and girls—among them, female infanticide (killing baby girls), genital mutilation, forced prostitution, widespread rape, and forced sterilization—in front of the full conference. Listeners applauded, cheered, and pounded their tables in support. At one point, her voice threaded with emotion, Hillary said, "If there is one message that echoes forth from this conference, let it be that human rights are women's rights, and women's rights are human rights, once and for all."

Her work reminded many of the role that First Lady Eleanor Roosevelt had chosen to play after leaving the White House. For many years, Roosevelt had written a newspaper column called My Day. Hillary revered Roosevelt. Modeling herself on her hero, she started writing her own weekly newspaper column in 1995, called Talking It Over. In this column, she discussed issues of concern to her, such as family life, education, and health care.

Of course, Hillary still had a job as a mother. Chelsea, then in high school, was getting ready to choose a college. She needed her mother's guidance and support.

Hillary began a new project. She decided to write a book about raising children in modern society. The book took its inspiration from an African saying, "It takes a village to raise a child." Hillary explained, "I chose that old African proverb [saying] to title this book because it offers a timeless reminder that children will thrive only if their families thrive and if the whole of society cares enough to provide for them."

When she wasn't traveling or appearing at special events, Hillary sat down to work on the book. She recorded her thoughts on children's health, education, and nutrition, and keeping children safe in a fast-paced, often troubled society. She wrote about ways that government could help children and parents, such as by funding child care programs and family leave (time off from work) for new parents. She completed the manuscript in late 1995, and the finished product, *It Takes a Village and Other Lessons Children Teach Us*, appeared on bookstore shelves in early 1996. Then Hillary set out across the country on a book-signing tour. People were eager to meet with her and buy her book. *It Takes a Village* became an immediate best-seller.

Though still haunted by scandals and investigations, Bill Clinton remained popular with a majority of the American people. In the Gallup organization's yearly poll, he had been named the Most Admired Man in the United States each year since taking office. (Hillary also won top honors as the

**Book tour:** Hillary shows off her book, *It Takes a Village*, in Washington, D.C., in 1996.

Most Admired Woman each year.) When he ran for president in 1996 against Republican Bob Dole, he again won by a wide margin. With the troubles of the first term behind them, Bill and Hillary were excited to continue their hard work on behalf of the American people.

Hillary won a Grammy Award for Best Spoken Word Album in 1997 for the audio version of *It Takes a Village.*

**Second parade:** Chelsea, Bill, and Hillary walk down Pennsylvania Avenue in Washington, D.C., during the inaugural parade in 1997.

# "This Vast Right-Wing Conspiracy"

The dawn of Bill Clinton's second term in office, winter 1997, was a positive time for the Clinton family. Chelsea was a senior in high school. She planned to attend Stanford University in California in the fall. In March 1997, Hillary and Chelsea took a trip to Africa, visiting several countries. During the trip, they came face-to-face with despair—such as the AIDS epidemic (widespread outbreak) that was devastating many

African nations and the thousands of children who were working instead of in school. And they came face-to-face with hope—such as the new democratic government in South Africa, where apartheid (the forced separation of blacks and whites) had recently ended.

As for Bill, he was confident that

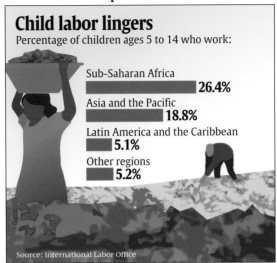

## USA TODAY Snapshots®

**Child labor lingers**
Percentage of children ages 5 to 14 who work:

Sub-Saharan Africa
**26.4%**
Asia and the Pacific
**18.8%**
Latin America and the Caribbean
**5.1%**
Other regions
**5.2%**

Source: International Labor Office

By David Stuckey and Alejandro Gonzalez, USA TODAY, 2007

his legal troubles were just about over. The Whitewater investigation, by then led by attorney Kenneth Starr, appeared to be winding down. Although several of the Clintons' former business partners had been charged with crimes, the Clintons had not been charged. Paula Jones dropped her lawsuit against Bill because they settled out of court. The president could finally get on with the business of running the country. As part of his new administration, he appointed Madeleine Albright secretary of state. She was the first woman ever to hold this position, one of the most important posts in the U.S. government.

## Household Transitions

In the spring of 1997, Chelsea Clinton graduated from Sidwell Friends School. The commencement speaker at her graduation ceremony was none other than the president of the United States—Bill Clinton. Later in the summer, the family vacationed on Martha's Vineyard in Massachusetts.

**College girl:** The Clintons exchange a laugh during welcome ceremonies at Stanford University in September 1997. Her parents helped Chelsea settle in for her freshman year of college in California.

When September arrived, both Bill and Hillary were glum. It was time for Chelsea to start college at Stanford. When Hillary had first learned that Chelsea wanted to go to Stanford, just south of San Francisco in California, she protested, "What! Stanford is too far away! You can't go that far away. That's all the way over on the West Coast— three time zones

# USA TODAY Snapshots®

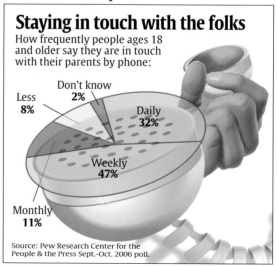

**Staying in touch with the folks**

How frequently people ages 18 and older say they are in touch with their parents by phone:

Don't know **2%**

Less **8%**

Daily **32%**

Weekly **47%**

Monthly **11%**

Source: Pew Research Center for the People & the Press Sept.-Oct. 2006 poll.

By Suzy Parker, USA TODAY, 2007

**September 19, 1997**

# Chelsea off to college

<u>From the Pages of</u>
<u>USA TODAY</u>

The first family joins parents across the nation today in a well-known ritual: taking their children to start their freshman year at college. As other parents know, it's a day filled with pride and pain. And today at Stanford University in Palo Alto, Calif., it's the Clinton family's turn. They'll leave their only child, 17-year-old Chelsea Victoria Clinton, at college. "I am dreading the moment Bill and I have to say good-bye to Chelsea," Hillary Clinton wrote in her syndicated newspaper column this week. "I know how great I should feel at her achievement and how excited I should be about the wonderful experiences that await her. But those are my mature moments. Most of the time, I'm wondering why I ever let her skip third grade."

—Mimi Hall

away." But by moving day, Hillary had calmed down. She was thrilled to see her daughter setting out on her own path. Bill and Hillary helped Chelsea settle in at her college dormitory and met some of her new college classmates.

When Bill and Hillary returned home, however, they were filled with loneliness. The solution, they decided, was to get a dog. Hillary located a three-month-old chocolate Labrador and presented him to Bill as a Christmas present. They decided to name him Buddy, after Bill's favorite uncle, who had recently died. The new puppy brightened Bill's and Hillary's spirits while they missed Chelsea. But one member of the household didn't like Buddy. Socks, the family cat, hissed whenever Buddy approached and once even swiped him on the nose.

## Old and New Demons

In January 1998, all Bill Clinton's legal troubles seemed to collapse into one another. That month Ken Starr, head of the Whitewater investigation team, expanded his investigation. In a turn of events that shocked and confused the public, Starr's team charged that during the Paula Jones sexual harassment case, Clinton had lied about a sexual affair with a young White House intern, Monica Lewinsky, and had asked Lewinsky to lie about the affair as well. Starr's legal team said that lying and encouraging Lewinsky to lie were impeachable offenses— Clinton could be removed from office if he were found guilty.

Hillary Clinton had heard it all before. She'd heard all the gossip about her husband's extramarital affairs. She'd heard all the false charges of Troopergate. The Lewinsky story, she assumed, was just another lie cooked up by Bill Clinton's Republican opponents to discredit him. What's more, Bill had told her all about the charges and assured

**Questions for the president:** In 1998 Whitewater investigator Ken Starr *(left)* accused Bill Clinton of having an affair with a White House intern, Monica Lewinsky *(right)*, and lying about it to investigators.

her they were untrue. He did know the young intern, he explained, but he certainly hadn't had an affair with her.

So when TV host Matt Lauer asked Hillary about the Lewinsky matter on the *Today* show one morning, Hillary was quick to give her take on the situation. First, she explained that, after five years as First Lady, she was quite used to unseemly rumors and the excitement that followed. "We're right in the middle of a rather vigorous feeding frenzy [media uproar] right now," she stated, "and people are saying all kinds of things and putting out rumor[s]. . . . And I have learned over the last many years being involved in politics, and especially since my husband first started running for President, that the best thing to do in these cases is just to be patient, take a deep breath and the truth will come out."

Then she went on to describe what she felt was the real source of the attacks against her husband. She said, "The great story here for anybody willing to find it and write about it and explain it is this vast right-wing conspiracy that has been conspiring against my husband since the day he announced for president."

A vast right-wing conspiracy? Had the right wing—that is, extreme conservatives—made up the Lewinsky story to disgrace Bill Clinton and then to bring impeachment charges against him? Hillary Clinton thought so.

She later described this conspiracy as "an interlocking network of groups and individuals who want to turn the clock back on many of the advances our country has made, from civil rights and women's rights to consumer and environmental regulation, and they use all the tools at their disposal—money, power, influence, media and politics—to achieve their ends. In recent years, they have also mastered the politics of personal destruction."

Many people agreed with Hillary. On February 9, *Newsweek* magazine published a chart outlining the financial and organizational links between conservative politicians, groups, and others; the various scandals associated with Clinton's presidency; and the Starr investigation. Soon after, David Brock, author of a 1994 magazine article that had stirred up the Troopergate scandal, admitted that he had been paid to write false accusations by groups determined to destroy Bill Clinton's presidency. Brock apologized to the president for his part in the incident.

## Confession

Despite this newest controversy, Bill Clinton continued to push forward with his agenda on national and international issues. In April he helped finalize a groundbreaking peace treaty in Northern Ireland, a region that had been torn apart by terrorism and religious conflict for centuries. Hillary immersed herself in her own work, such as the Save America's Treasures program, a project to protect and restore revered artifacts of U.S. history, such as the flag that inspired the writing of the "The Star-Spangled Banner," the U.S. national anthem.

Then, on the morning of August 15, Bill woke Hillary with some shocking news. Pacing back and forth in their bedroom, he admitted that the Monica Lewinsky rumors were true. He had had a brief affair with the young woman, he confessed. Hillary was angry and heartbroken. Two days after confessing to his wife, Bill addressed the nation on television and made the same confession. In his speech, he apologized for his behavior but defended his right to privacy.

As Hillary struggled to come to terms with her husband's betrayal, the media uproar got even louder. Republicans called for Bill Clinton's impeachment. Some called for his resignation. Most Democrats felt that Clinton should be reprimanded (denounced) for his affair with Lewinsky but that impeachment was not fitting. He had made a terrible mistake, true, but his private actions certainly hadn't harmed the government or the American people. Historians and constitutional scholars agreed that Bill Clinton's offenses were not grounds for impeachment.

Hillary remained hurt and angry at her husband, but she also argued that his mistakes were a private matter and certainly not punishable by impeachment. And even though her husband had lied to her, she stood by her claim that a right-wing network was trying to destroy his presidency.

**November 24, 1998**

## A regal renaissance for first lady

From the Pages of **USA TODAY**

The hard-fought comeback of Hillary Rodham Clinton is on display this week with the arrival of the December issue of *Vogue* magazine. On the cover, instead of a supermodel or a Hollywood star, is the first lady, in a burgundy Oscar de la Renta evening gown, in the Red Room of the White House. She is the picture of poise and elegance.

Nearly a year after the story of her husband's affair with onetime intern Monica Lewinsky made headlines worldwide, here's Hillary Clinton: the wronged wife looking more than all right, the weakened woman who somehow seems stronger. "She's come out of a disgusting situation, frankly, with incredible grace," *Vogue* editor Anna Wintour says. "She behaved with intelligence and dignity. We felt, in a way, she was our woman of the year."

The *Vogue* cover comes after an election season that saw Hillary Clinton rise to the political occasion and take her husband's place on the campaign trail. He may have been hobbled by scandal, but she didn't hold back. She stumped for Democratic candidates coast to coast and was credited with helping re-energize voters who were turned off by just about everything happening in Washington.

It was the culmination of a reinvention. Four years ago, polls found the country split on Hillary Clinton. She was seen by some as a self-appointed co-president whose elaborate plan to reform the health insurance system died of its own weight. She was at the center of several ethics controversies, including legal work on the Whitewater land deal. Polls found her favorable ratings in the mid-40s. Ten months ago, she was the betrayed, pitied wife. Since then, her ratings have been 60% or better.

—Mimi Hall

The American public seemed to be mostly on President Clinton's side. Although few could excuse his private behavior, about 60 percent of Americans polled said that Clinton should not be impeached for his actions, nor did they think he should resign. Interestingly, Hillary Clinton's approval ratings (a measure of the public's support for her) improved during this period. It appeared that people around the country sympathized with her personal problems.

However, many people, especially women, wondered how she could stay with a cheating husband. In fact, Hillary did consider leaving Bill, but she took her time deciding. She and Bill began marital counseling after he came clean about the Lewinsky affair. Hillary

**First family:** Hillary, Chelsea, Bill, and Buddy make their first public appearance in August 1998 after Bill admitted to having a sexual relationship with Monica Lewinsky.

also spoke privately with Donald Jones, her youth minister from her teenage years in Illinois who had become a lifelong friend. After long weeks of soul-searching, Hillary decided to stick with her marriage to Bill and try to improve their relationship.

Meanwhile, the impeachment process moved forward. On September 9, Kenneth Starr delivered a 445-page report to Congress describing Bill Clinton's affair with Monica Lewinsky. The original cause of the investigation, Whitewater, was barely mentioned in the report. In December the U.S. House of Representatives impeached the president on two charges: perjury (lying under oath) and obstruction of justice (blocking the progress of a legal case). Finding the president guilty of these charges and removing him from office would require a two-thirds vote of the Senate. The highly publicized impeachment trial started on January 7, 1999, and lasted five weeks. In February the Senate found Clinton not guilty, and he served out his term as president.

Meanwhile, he continued to do his job. For example, he tried to negotiate a peace agreement between Israeli prime minister Ehud Barak and Palestinian leader Yasser Arafat. But Clinton's reputation was stained, and his marriage was strained. His two terms had been scarred by scandal and political mudslinging. In 2000, when Vice President Al Gore ran for president, Gore deliberately distanced himself from his former running mate.

# IN FOCUS

## Impeachment

Impeachment is a complicated process for essentially firing a U.S. president while the person is in office. It's a serious matter and isn't meant to be easily accomplished. The U.S. Constitution says a president can only be impeached by being convicted for committing treason, bribery, or other high crimes and misdemeanors.

Both parts of the U.S. Congress—the House of Representatives and the Senate—have roles in the impeachment process. Two-thirds of the members of the House must vote in favor of accusing the president of impeachable charges. The Senate then tries the president on these charges. Two-thirds of the Senate must vote to convict the president of the charges for the president to be removed from office.

**Running on her own:** Hillary announces her candidacy for senator from New York at a press conference in February 2000. She is surrounded by Democratic politicians from New York, as well as her family (*right side of photo, second from left*), Bill, Chelsea, and Hillary's mother, Dorothy Rodham.

# Senator Clinton

The 2000 presidential race featured Democrat Al Gore, Bill Clinton's vice president, against Republican George W. Bush, son of the first President George Bush. The race was expected to be close. Americans and the media followed the conventions, campaign speeches, political advertisements, and candidate debates with interest.

## Taking New York by Storm

Another intriguing campaign was under way that year: Hillary Clinton's run for Senate in

New York. After moving to New York to establish residency and then winning her party's nomination in mid-May, Clinton hit the campaign trail. Chelsea took time off from school to help her mother campaign. Clinton's original opponent, Mayor Rudolph Giuliani, had dropped out of the race due to health concerns. Her new opponent was Republican congressman Rick Lazio.

Lazio tried some negative campaigning. He tried to paint Clinton as a "pushy" feminist. He called her a carpetbagger because she had moved to New York only a month before the race began. He tried to convince New York's Jewish voters that she didn't support the Jewish state of Israel. He even made an outrageous accusation that she had links to a Middle Eastern terrorist organization.

But Clinton never attacked Lazio in return. She stuck to issues that New York voters cared about: jobs, health care, opportunities for minorities, and the environment. She spent a lot of time in rural upstate New York, learning about the issues that troubled farmers and

**Debate 2000:** Hillary gets ready for her final debate with New York Republican congressman Rick Lazio *(left)* in October 2000. Also pictured is NBC journalist Gabe Pressman, the moderator of the debate.

small-town citizens there. She spent time in Manhattan, listening to the concerns of city dwellers. She attended community events and visited college campuses. Voters everywhere lined up to meet her, and they liked what they heard and saw. And rather than finding her "pushy," many voters—especially women—loved her strength and her support for family, children, and health-care issues.

Clinton took a lead over Lazio in the polls. When election day came, she beat out Lazio 55 percent to 43 percent, becoming the only First Lady ever to win an elected public office. The family was joyful, but it was hard to be completely upbeat. The presidential race had a rocky ending. After a too-close-to-call vote in Florida and a subsequent dispute over recounting the ballots there, the U.S. Supreme Court named George W. Bush the winner of the 2000 presidential election. Despite Hillary Clinton's victory, it was a dark time for the Democratic Party.

## At Work in Washington

Hillary Clinton was sworn in as a member of the U.S. Senate on January 3, 2001. For twenty-five years, she had played a supporting role in her husband's political career. Finally, it was her turn to take the lead.

**Senator from New York:** Bill holds the Bible as Hillary is sworn in to the U.S. Senate by Vice President Al Gore in January 2001. Chelsea was also there to support her mother.

Along with a staff of twenty-seven, she settled into an office on the fourth floor of the Russell Senate Office Building in Washington, D.C. She and Bill also bought and renovated a six-bedroom, $2.9 million house in an exclusive Washington, D.C., neighborhood. This would be Hillary's home when she worked in the nation's capital. Her mother, Dorothy Rodham, would live there too. When her schedule allowed, Hillary would return to her house in Chappaqua, New York.

During the early months of 2001, Hillary Clinton watched and learned. As a brand-new elected official and one of one hundred senators, she didn't have much clout, or influence, in the Senate. And some people predicted that Republican senators who hadn't liked her husband wouldn't like her either. But she remained enthusiastic. "I have worked with a number of Republican [Senate] members in the past," she said. "I'm looking forward to working with them on a bipartisan [two parties working together] basis on issues that affect their states, as well as New York, and of course our entire country."

Clinton began her work in the Senate by introducing bills that would benefit New Yorkers, especially those in rural areas. The first bill she presented helped rural communities get broadband (high-speed) communications access. Another bill involved the building of a new $100 million border-crossing station between upstate New York and Canada.

Clinton showed herself to be focused and a fast learner. She impressed other senators with her command of the issues that came to the Senate for consideration. Even Republicans praised her. Republican senator Trent Lott, who had frequently fought with President Clinton and made negative remarks about Hillary during her Senate campaign, was impressed by the new senator from New York. He saw her as a hard worker who didn't try to use her fame as a former First Lady to her advantage. "I think she's doing fine," he said. "I think she's trying to dig in and do her homework, trying to lower her profile a little bit." Clinton also teamed up with several Republican senators to sponsor legislation in areas ranging from military spending to nursing.

## July 10, 2001

# Hillary Clinton building legacy of her own

### From the Pages of USA TODAY

Six months after taking her seat in the Senate amid a storm of controversy over her husband's last-minute pardons and the furniture they moved from the White House, one of the most controversial first ladies in history is enjoying a political honeymoon. Even from her political critics, Clinton is winning respect as a hard-working, low-key legislator.

The woman many predicted would be too big for Congress is surprising denizens of Capitol Hill with how well she fits in. Her Secret Service detail is unobtrusive. In the bustling halls of the Capitol, Clinton rubs shoulders with curious tourists, swaps tips with other female senators on such burning questions as the best totes (briefcase or big purse?), even touches up her lipstick in front of reporters.

At 53, the once proudly private Clinton now relishes her public role. "I like it because I have an actual job to do, where what I'm doing is really the most important thing to the public," she says. "If anything, the public attention is sort of diminishing, which is fine with me. But when it does come, it comes because of what I'm actually doing, and I like that."

"I think Hillary Clinton has really worked hard to do her job and not create a lot of attention—just to be a senator like everybody else. And that's very difficult for her," says Sen. Bob Smith, R-N.H., one of Clinton's colleagues on the Environment and Public Works Committee. "But I think people just view her now as a colleague—not the ex-first lady, but a senator."

Smith is one of a number of staunch conservatives who, despite sharp political differences with the New York Democrat, have found Clinton a genial colleague. Sens. Sam Brownback, R-Kan., James Inhofe, R-Okla., and John Ensign, R-Nev., have all co-sponsored legislation with her. She and Sen. Orrin Hatch, R-Utah, chaired a charity fundraiser together.

—Kathy Kiely

## The New World at War

September 11, 2001 (9/11), was a dark day for the nation and especially for New York City. On that day, terrorists hijacked four airplanes and crashed two of them into the World Trade Center towers in New York City and another into the Pentagon, the U.S. military headquarters near Washington, D.C. A fourth plane, likely bound for the U.S. Capitol, crashed in the Pennsylvania countryside after passengers struggled with the hijackers. Altogether, about three thousand people were killed in the attacks.

In New York City, the two World Trade Center towers burned and then collapsed. The damage was massive. Ground Zero—the site of the collapsed towers—looked like a war zone. Along with fellow New York senator Charles Schumer, Clinton was at the forefront of helping the city recover. She and Schumer secured $21.4 billion in federal funding to help New Yorkers clean up and rebuild at Ground Zero. She also provided much-needed emotional support to New Yorkers, especially those who had lost family members in the attack.

With the September 11 attacks, the United States found itself at war. First, the United States invaded Afghanistan, whose government had provided a safe haven for the 9/11 terrorists. Next, in early 2003, the United States invaded Iraq, in part because President Bush said he believed that Iraq was stockpiling weapons of mass destruction (nuclear, biological, and chemical weapons).

Senator Clinton voted in favor of the Iraq invasion. But once U.S. troops had occupied Iraq, she criticized the way the administration was carrying out the war. She saw that President Bush was pumping billions and billions of dollars into the war in Iraq while at the same time cutting programs such as education and social services at home. In addition, soon after the war began, it became clear that Iraq had no weapons of mass destruction—Bush's original argument for invading Iraq had been based on faulty information. Along with other Democrats in Congress, Clinton voiced her opposition to the president's policies in Iraq.

## Looking Back and Forward

While Senator Clinton was helping the nation through the difficult new "war on terrorism," she also took time to reflect on the past. On nights and weekends, she completed a 534-page autobiography called *Living History*. The book examines her life to the year 2001, from her childhood in Illinois through the Clinton presidency to her run for Senate. Creating the book was a massive project that required the help of ghostwriters—professional authors who did much of the writing based on Hillary's notes and recollections.

Released in June 2003, the book sold more than one million copies in the first month after publication. It was translated into thirty-five languages and distributed around the world.

*Living History:* Hillary signs copies of her autobiography, *Living History*, at an event in New York City in June 2003.

Hillary Clinton was more popular than ever. Many wondered if Hillary might be thinking about entering the presidential race in 2004. She continued to say that she was committed to finishing her six-year term in the Senate. Some political observers believed her, but some didn't.

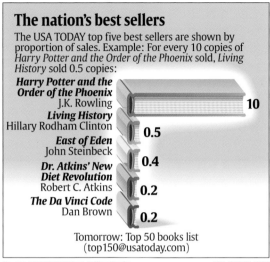

USA TODAY Snapshots®

**The nation's best sellers**

The USA TODAY top five best sellers are shown by proportion of sales. Example: For every 10 copies of *Harry Potter and the Order of the Phoenix* sold, *Living History* sold 0.5 copies:

*Harry Potter and the Order of the Phoenix*
J.K. Rowling — **10**

*Living History*
Hillary Rodham Clinton — **0.5**

*East of Eden*
John Steinbeck — **0.4**

*Dr. Atkins' New Diet Revolution*
Robert C. Atkins — **0.2**

*The Da Vinci Code*
Dan Brown — **0.2**

Tomorrow: Top 50 books list (top150@usatoday.com)

Source: USA TODAY Best-Selling Books          USA TODAY, 2003

In the Senate, Hillary joined the Senate Armed Services Committee (she already sat on the Environment and Public Works Committee and the Health, Education, Labor, and Pensions Committee). The Armed Services Committee is the group of senators who study bills related to military and defense issues. Clinton wanted to serve on the committee because she thought the nation was spending too much money on war and too little on other important projects. She explained:

> I concluded that the war on terrorism is a long-term challenge, and that it will be important to understand what our military response will be and to satisfy myself we're as well defended as we need to be. It's also very clear that [the Bush] Administration has a strategy to starve the federal budget of everything but defense. I think that's a mistake to turn our backs on so many of our important domestic and international priorities. . . . I wanted to have some understanding and influence over how that money [the federal budget] was going to be spent.

## September 23, 2003

# How firm is Hillary's no?

From the Pages of
USA TODAY

She has two Web sites urging her to run for president, a husband dropping hints and a media buzz that won't quit. But Hillary Rodham Clinton is still saying what she said a year ago: She's going to be a senator from New York at least until January 2007, when her term expires.

A new poll shows two-thirds of Clinton's constituents believe her when she says she won't run for the White House in 2004, up from half in December 2000. That's a testament to her own denials and the statement her spokesman, Philippe Reines, sends to anyone who asks: "Sen. Clinton has repeatedly said that she will serve out her full six-year term. She loves her job and is working on being the best senator she can be for the people of New York."

Speculation nevertheless persists in tabloids, on cable TV and among some columnists. It's rooted in Clinton's fame, Democratic fantasies and a large field without a clear front-runner. Then there's the fodder from the Clinton camp itself that keeps hope alive. E-mails on the senator's re-election site (friendsofhillary.com) urging her to run for president in 2004 and 2008. The e-mails, part of a sampling of responses to a newsletter, were removed Friday. "We don't want anyone to be confused," Reines said. Then there's votehillary.org, a draft-Hillary site complete with petition and plans for a Nov. 1 rally on Capitol Hill. "I don't think any of the other candidates can actually pull in the votes" to beat President Bush, said founder Adam Parkhomenko, a student at Northern Virginia Community College.

—Jill Lawrence

During the Thanksgiving holiday in 2003, Clinton visited U.S. troops in Afghanistan and Iraq. She wanted to see firsthand what the soldiers fighting in the Middle East were going through. She paid special attention to troops who hailed from New York. Back at home, she devoted much of her work on the Armed Services Committee to

**Meet and greet:** Hillary visited U.S. troops in Afghanistan and Iraq in November 2003. Here she shakes hands with a soldier at an air base outside Kabul, Afghanistan.

fighting for benefits and health care for military veterans.

In 2004 Clinton became chairperson of the Senate's Democratic Steering Committee—an association of Democrats in the Senate. She also helped create the Center for American Progress, a liberal think tank (research organization). These efforts positioned her well within her own party. Meanwhile, she worked with other senators—both Republican and Democrat—to push for laws to expand health care, to modernize and digitize the health-care system, and to fine video game producers if they didn't appropriately rate their games intended for sale for children. Although she voted for increases in the number of U.S. ground troops in Iraq, Clinton also continued to criticize the Bush administration for its handling of the war.

Meanwhile, Bill Clinton published his memoir, *My Life*. It chronicled his early life and schooling, as well as some of his personal mistakes. Some reviewers and readers felt it was a public apology to Hillary for all she'd endured as his wife. Some even felt the book boosted Hillary's celebrity and her prospects as a viable future candidate for president. She stayed quiet about the subject.

## June 23, 2004

# *My Life* may give Hillary a boost

<u>From the Pages of USA TODAY</u>

Former president Bill Clinton says he didn't write his memoir with his wife's political future in mind, but his just-released *My Life* makes it clear that he is New York Sen. Hillary Rodham Clinton's biggest political booster. "I always believed she had as much (or more) potential to succeed in politics as I did," Clinton writes in his memoir. "I wanted her to have her chance."

For the ex-president, the former first lady's improbable journey into elective politics represents what could be the most historic aspect of his White House legacy. Though she has said that her only political ambition is to serve her constituents, Clinton stands the best chance of any woman in history to become president. She already has the fundraising ability, the constituency and the celebrity wattage to make her a formidable national contender. Political leaders across the ideological spectrum assume she's a front-runner for the Democratic presidential nomination four years from now if John Kerry fails to unseat President Bush this year.

Many political observers think that her husband's book will enhance Clinton's image as much as her own best-selling memoir, *Living History*, did a year ago. Hillary Clinton is cast as a heroine of her husband's *Life*. He portrays his wife as a stalwart helpmate who gave him good advice and stood up for him even when he didn't deserve it. Recalling her appearance on national television the day after the story of his affair with White House intern Monica Lewinsky broke, Clinton writes: "Seeing Hillary defend me made me even more ashamed about what I had done." The book is a public letter of apology to his wife, of whom Clinton says: "I had always loved her very much, but not always very well."

As her husband carries on with his book tour this summer, Hillary Clinton will be busy with her own political career. She's hosting a party at her Washington home today for Barack Obama, the Democratic candidate for Senate in Illinois. Next week, she heads to the West Coast to raise money for Sens. Barbara Boxer, D-Calif., and Patty Murray, D-Wash. On June 30, she'll co-host a New York City fundraiser for the Democratic Senatorial Campaign Committee that's expected to net $2 million. Over the past 15 months, Clinton has participated in more than 50 events for candidates, including three for Kerry.

—Kathy Kiely

**Official portraits:** Bill and Hillary visited the White House in June 2004 for the unveiling of their official portraits, which will hang in the White House. Bill's autobiography, *My Life*, also came out that year.

## Establishing Herself

Hillary easily won reelection in 2006, with 67 percent of the vote. Her campaign cost around thirty-six million dollars. Some criticized her for spending so much on a contest she was likely to win. But that criticism didn't diminish her popularity—even among frugal-minded Republicans.

Clinton's voting record in the Senate further established her views for many U.S. citizens, whether they supported her or not. In 2007 she opposed an increase in the number of troops being sent to Iraq. General David Petraeus, who was overseeing military operations in that region, introduced this tactic for handling the war, known as a surge. Clinton and many other Democrats felt that the army was stretched to the limit. They believed it was time to start bringing troops home not sending more.

Another pressing issue for Clinton and other politicians was the state of the U.S. economy. Many banks were failing because they had been carelessly lending money to people who could not pay it back.

## November 9, 2006

# Elections help sort out playing field for 2008

From the Pages of
USA TODAY
The elections this week transformed not only Congress but the playing field for the 2008 presidential race. Some contenders self-destructed, one went home and a meteor streaked onto the radar in the form of Illinois Sen. Barack Obama.

There were two things, however, that didn't change: the contenders leading the polls on both sides.

Sen. Hillary Rodham Clinton, D-N.Y., won a resounding re-election victory after raising nearly $40 million—more than any other Senate candidate this year. She isn't yet talking about her future, which is widely presumed to include a presidential bid but could involve a leadership role in a possibly Democratic Senate.

Some analysts praise her campaign skills but say they wouldn't be surprised if she chooses the latter, given the difficulties of a White House run.

The Republican front-runner, Arizona Sen. John McCain, campaigned and raised money for candidates nationwide while also building a network for his White House bid. Though supportive of President Bush on Iraq, his disagreements with Bush about immigration policy, prisoner abuse and Defense Secretary Donald Rumsfeld's performance kept his maverick image alive.

Two red-state Democrats, former North Carolina senator John Edwards and Indiana Sen. Evan Bayh, solidified their standing in ways that may pay off later.

Edwards fought for minimum-wage hikes and strengthened ties with labor. Bayh helped Indiana Democrats oust three House Republicans and helped Democrats capture the legislature in Iowa, a key primary-season state. Illinois' Obama, who is half Kansan and half Kenyan, generated big crowds even as his short resume raised questions. If the freshman senator decides to proceed, says Squire, "he's going to find out that it's a tough business. He's had the fun part already, and the painful part is coming up."

—Jill Lawrence

Eventually, these people could not afford their monthly mortgage payments and found themselves struggling to hold on to their homes. The number of foreclosures—the legal procedure for banks to take back property after someone defaults on their mortgage payments—rose alarmingly. As a result, banks stopped lending as much, and fewer people could afford to buy property. Prices in real estate began to plunge because few people were buying. Almost everyone who had widely invested in property was losing a lot of money.

The overall effect was that the U.S. dollar began to lose its value and that fewer foreign countries were willing to invest in U.S. companies. Some of the largest banks in the nation began to fail, and many Americans lost their jobs. Small businesses were particularly hard hit.

In addition to the economy and the Iraq War, many politicians, including Clinton, had growing concerns about the U.S. health-care system. Many Americans had no health insurance. If they became sick or injured, they would have to pay the bills out of pocket. People often found themselves dealing with their health and their finances at the same time. Clinton, who as First Lady had championed health-care reform, took a keen interest in this revived call for action on this issue.

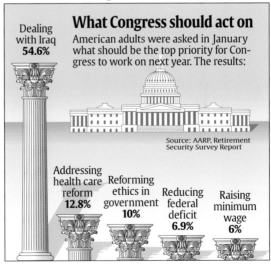

By David Stuckey and Bob Laird, USA TODAY, 2007

**www.usatoday.com**

**USA TODAY**

**CHAPTER NINE**

**Running on her own:** Hillary campaigns in Iowa in January 2007. She competed against other Democrats for the nomination for president through 2007 and part of 2008.

# A Challenging Race

On January 20, 2007—two years before the next president would be sworn into office—Clinton announced her candidacy for the job. She declared "I'm in and I'm in to win!" She saw an opportunity to steer the country in a new direction, and she had a lot of momentum behind her.

As a senator, she had gained solid experience with foreign policy.

Because of Bill Clinton's popularity, many voters identified the prosperity during his presidency with her. Although some people viewed Hillary as a polarizing figure—meaning people either loved or hated her—she was still consistently ranked as one of the most respected women in the United States. With all of these assets, many Democrats viewed her as the natural presidential nominee for their party. Polling in January of 2007 placed her far ahead of other contenders.

But Clinton was not the only rising star in the upcoming presidential election. Barack Obama, a young first-term senator from Illinois, became Hillary's biggest rival for the presidency. Obama first made a name for himself delivering the keynote address at the 2004 Democratic National Convention. Many found his speech inspiring, and he soon came to represent the change that many Americans wanted in politics.

Through the spring of 2007, Democrats and Republicans competed in primary elections in various states to show who had the broadest national support to become each party's nominee for president. Potential nominees participated in debates to showcase their positions on the issues and to drum up support. Clinton traveled the country making her case that she was the best candidate for the job. Among her Democratic rivals were Obama, Senator Chris Dodd of Connecticut, and former senator John Edwards. Eventually, Dodd, Edwards, and other contenders withdrew.

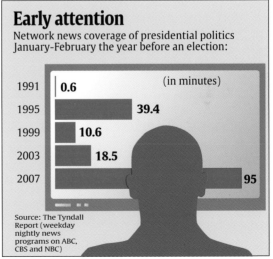

USA TODAY Snapshots®

**Early attention**
Network news coverage of presidential politics January-February the year before an election:

(in minutes)

| Year | Minutes |
|------|---------|
| 1991 | 0.6 |
| 1995 | 39.4 |
| 1999 | 10.6 |
| 2003 | 18.5 |
| 2007 | 95 |

Source: The Tyndall Report (weekday nightly news programs on ABC, CBS and NBC)

By Adrienne Lewis, USA TODAY, 2007

**January 22, 2007**

# Why some Democrats worry that she can't win

<u>From the Pages of</u>
<u>USA TODAY</u>
She's a celebrity with an impressive resume, major-league supporters and five consecutive years of being the Gallup Poll's "most admired woman." Yet as New York Sen. Hillary Rodham Clinton plunges into the race for the Democratic presidential nomination, she faces resistance from fellow Democrats who don't like her, don't like her positions on issues or don't think she can win.

Clinton is a complicated package. Her constituents and Senate colleagues generally view her as smart and hard-working. On the challenge side of the ledger, there's her personality (perceived in some quarters as chilly), her vote on Iraq (she supported the war) and her gender (are Americans ready for a female president?). Then there's that husband of hers. Could there be a more complicated marriage in America?

"She doesn't fit the mold," says Elizabeth Ossoff, a political psychologist at St. Anselm's College in Manchester, N.H. She predicts "a difficult but very interesting race. A lot of things are going to get brought up, and people are going to have to face their opinions."

—Jill Lawrence

The choice of nominee came down to Clinton or Obama. Either winner would be a first for the United States. Clinton would be the first female nominee. Obama would be the first African American nominee. Many women voters looked up to Hillary as a strong and intelligent female leader. She also had strong Hispanic support. Hillary's Senate voting record on health care, the economy, and the war in Iraq also made her quite popular among the working class and unions. She seemed poised to win the nomination.

On the other hand, Obama had a very strong following among the younger generation of voters and among African Americans. The two candidates each had roughly half of the Democratic Party's traditional supporters. Even those who did not identify themselves as Democrats found themselves drawn in.

## Making an Impression

Clinton earned early criticism that her strength and determination made her come

**Democratic debaters:** Barack Obama and Hillary faced off for many debates during the course of the 2007–2008 primary season.

across as cold and unfeeling. She then tried to balance her public persona between being an aggressive candidate and a likable one. One adviser, Mark J. Penn, was pushing for Hillary to be more forceful. Penn had masterminded Bill Clinton's 1996 reelection campaign and had become a close family friend. His opinion within the Hillary campaign was well respected.

However, others on staff were more interested in adopting the sunny approach that Obama had been using with success. They worried that if Hillary was too aggressive, her image would be damaged.

While Hillary's camp was divided as to what course to take, Obama's well-organized campaign was making strides. In February of 2008, Hillary suffered a losing streak. Obama won the contests in Louisiana, Washington, Nebraska, Maine, Maryland, Virginia, and the District of Columbia. His support seemed to be building.

But Hillary Clinton's determination kept her in the race. After getting a bruising in February, Hillary decided to give Mark Penn's aggressive approach a shot. Her campaign aired a television ad that showed children sleeping peacefully while the narrator asks viewers whom they trusted to handle the country during an emergency. The implication was that Hillary, with her knowledge of world af-

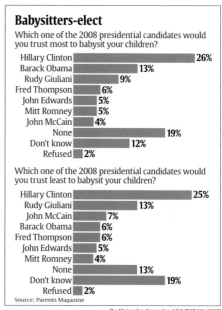

**Babysitters-elect**

Which one of the 2008 presidential candidates would you trust most to babysit your children?

| | |
|---|---|
| Hillary Clinton | 26% |
| Barack Obama | 13% |
| Rudy Giuliani | 9% |
| Fred Thompson | 6% |
| John Edwards | 5% |
| Mitt Romney | 5% |
| John McCain | 4% |
| None | 19% |
| Don't know | 12% |
| Refused | 2% |

Which one of the 2008 presidential candidates would you trust least to babysit your children?

| | |
|---|---|
| Hillary Clinton | 25% |
| Rudy Giuliani | 13% |
| John McCain | 7% |
| Barack Obama | 6% |
| Fred Thompson | 6% |
| John Edwards | 5% |
| Mitt Romney | 4% |
| None | 13% |
| Don't know | 19% |
| Refused | 2% |

Source: Parents Magazine

By Alejandro Gonzalez, USA TODAY, 2007

fairs, would be better suited to answer the call. Some people thought that the ad was too negative and that it suggested that Obama was someone not to be trusted. However, the ad seemed to be effective, because thereafter Hillary won in Texas and Ohio. She had come back from the brink of defeat.

A pattern was emerging in Hillary Clinton's campaign. As soon as her bid for the nomination looked all but lost, she would win another primary. Many other politicians would have been shaken. But Hillary's experiences had made her resilient—a quality that supporters and even some of her detractors admired.

## Bill on Board

The spring of 2008 found Hillary Clinton's presidential campaign yet again on the ropes. Although she held her own at every debate and demonstrated herself to be one of the most knowledgeable candidates, Obama's appeal to voters was gaining every day. Not since Bill Clinton had there been a candidate who possessed such winning charisma and the ability to inspire others. With that in mind, some advisers suggested having Bill himself campaign for her. Mark J. Penn especially pushed for this idea.

Many within her campaign, including the Clintons themselves, were concerned about associating Hillary too much with Bill. Bill Clinton was the Democratic Party's rock star. His appeal was worldwide. How could Bill use his popularity to help Hillary without overshadowing her? Would voters lose sight of Hillary's strengths and accomplishments if Bill joined the show?

All through Bill Clinton's presidential campaigns, the couple had successfully marketed themselves as two for the price of one. If it had worked then, why shouldn't it work now? With this in mind, Bill Clinton set out across the country giving speeches for Hillary wherever he went and drawing large crowds. He also talked privately with superdelegates whose votes at the Democratic National Convention in Denver, Colorado, would help decide who won the nomination.

**Campaigning for Hillary:** Bill and Chelsea campaigned for Hillary all across the United States. Here they attend a rally in Oklahoma in 2008.

Bill Clinton also compared Obama's campaign to that of the Reverend Jesse Jackson in 1984. Jackson, a well-respected African American civil rights leader, had not won his party's nomination. Some felt that Bill Clinton was suggesting that Obama's campaign would also fail because, like Jackson, he was a person of color. Bill Clinton, for his part, insisted he meant no such thing, but

other similar gaffes led many to worry that he was losing Hillary support from the African American community. In addition, many were
concerned about a copresidency. Would Bill run the country alongside
Hillary if she were president?

Chelsea Clinton followed in her father's footsteps by campaigning
for her mother. She toured the country, appearing especially at gather-
ings on college campuses. As a daughter, she knew her mother almost
better than anyone. She could give people a way of viewing Hillary that
was warm and personal. Voters heard childhood stories from Chelsea,
ranging from Christmas memories to her love of the children's book
*Goodnight Moon.*

## A Campaign Divided

Despite a united family front, further conflicts emerged within Hillary's campaign group. Friction existed between her staff and her husband's. Some of Bill Clinton's staff felt that he should have more say
about decisions because of his success as a politician and world leader.
Many on Hillary's staff felt that Bill's aides were overstepping their positions. They worried that Hillary Clinton was being undermined. The
couple seemed to get along fine throughout the campaign, but their
closest supporters had begun to split into competing groups.

To make matters worse, Penn's ideas were alarming many campaign workers. Penn wanted the Hillary campaign to highlight in a
negative way Obama's diverse upbringing. Obama's father was from
Kenya, and his stepfather was from Indonesia, a predominantly Muslim
country, where Obama had gone to school as a boy. Penn felt if voters
were focused on Obama's background, he would seem less American
to them. This would allow Hillary to cast herself as the candidate who
more represented American values.

Many within Hillary's campaign felt that it was wrong to portray
cultural diversity as a bad thing. After all, wasn't the United States sup-
posed to be the great melting pot of the world? But because Penn had
played such a key role in reelecting Bill Clinton, many were worried

**Hillary fans:** Hillary hugs a supporter during the New York primary in February 2008.

about contradicting him. To her credit, Hillary decided to shy away from focusing on Obama's roots in such a manner. But the damage from internal fighting was done. While her campaign had been in conflict with itself, Obama had continued to raise money at a staggering rate. By April 2008, Hillary's campaign was severely in debt.

Meanwhile, questions about Hillary's honesty emerged. They stemmed from her description of a trip to Bosnia she'd taken when she was First Lady. She claimed that she landed amid gunfire and that she had to run with her head down to avoid being shot by snipers. However, video footage later showed her walking calmly off the plane with Chelsea. Nothing dangerous about the landing showed up in the video. Hillary claimed she had misspoken. But many voters began to distrust her after this incident.

Whether or not people viewed her as trustworthy, Hillary Clinton still won the Pennsylvania primary. She remained a very strong contender among working-class Americans. Her frank approach to discussing the economic issues facing the nation appealed to those who had lost their jobs or were faced with that prospect. For these voters, Obama's message of hope sounded nice but did not address their concerns.

**May 8, 2008**

# Not just any woman

From the Pages of
USA TODAY

In recent weeks, Clinton seems to have picked up a Y chromosome somewhere and morphed into the manliest of Democrats. The candidate who initially aimed for the women's vote, calling her campaign a "conversation" and convening "chats," has suddenly swilled beer and Crown Royal chasers with boys in the bar, stumped from pickups and displayed her "testicular fortitude," as an Indiana labor leader recently described her.

The women's vote, meanwhile, has splintered. Important feminist leaders—including Susan Sarandon, *Nation* columnist Katha Pollitt and women's rights historians Alice Kessler-Harris and Linda Gordon—side with Barack Obama. And black women vote overwhelmingly for the black candidate (about 80%). What happened? Though Clinton has done well with women—who have constituted about 60% of voters in Democratic primaries—why aren't more of them supporting the first woman with a shot at the presidency? Or are these questions not really the right ones to ask? Is it possible that it isn't A Woman voters are rejecting, but a particular woman? Is it possible Clinton is the wrong candidate, who just happens to be a woman?

Clinton is the tough, gritty pugilist who makes "Rocky Balboa look like a pansy," according to North Carolina Gov. Mike Easley. She's the one who voted for the war in Iraq and who has promised annihilation to Iran should that country attack Israel. "I'm not going to put my lot in with economists," she said on ABC's *This Week* when asked for the name of an economist who agrees with her proposed gas-tax summer vacation. And then: "Elite opinion is always on the side of doing things that really disadvantages the vast majority of Americans." Bring 'em on, sister! Elitism sucketh.

If Clinton loses, it won't be because women betrayed her. It will be because Obama offered something that women—and men—want more. A fresh start free of tired tropes and battered baggage. Giving Clinton her due, she has made history. She got up every day and kept smiling. She looked good and sometimes great, and older women marveled at her stamina. Not least, she prevailed in nearly every debate.

But her losses are her own.

—Kathleen Parker, from the Opinion page

Setting aside the division within her campaign, Hillary Clinton found the voice with which she was most comfortable. She stopped reacting to Obama's popularity or trying to find the right balance between aggressive and likable. Instead, she rekindled the earnest conversation with the American people that she had used at the beginning of her campaign. She addressed their problems and demonstrated she knew what the country was going through.

Shortly after winning in Pennsylvania, Hillary gave a speech. It struck the note that would signal the best she had to offer as a candidate. "With two wars abroad and an economic crisis here at home, you know the stakes are high and the challenges are great, but you also know the possibilities. Those possibilities are endless if we roll up our sleeves and get to work with a president who's ready to lead on day one."

Competence was a quality that many voters felt was lacking in George W. Bush and was untested in Barack Obama. The same was difficult to say about Hillary Clinton. Supporters and detractors recognized her abilities. Her competence became her foremost argument behind her candidacy as the Democratic race headed into the summer months. Meanwhile, the Republicans had all but chosen John McCain to be their nominee.

Hillary won the primaries in Indiana, West Virginia, Kentucky, and Puerto Rico. More important, she won in key states with large delegate counts, such as Texas, Ohio, California, and New York. Yet, at the same time, Obama was racking up delegates that pushed him ever closer to the number he needed to earn the nomination of the Democratic Party.

## A Strong Finish

The strong voice of Hillary's supporters and her trademark competitive spirit made it extremely hard for Hillary to concede the nomination. Everywhere she went, Hillary was encouraged not to drop out and to keep fighting for them. With 18 million votes cast for her, the

www.usatoday.com

**USA TODAY**

# News

SECTION A

**May 14, 2008**

# Blowout bolsters Clinton resolve

<u>From the Pages of</u>
<u>USA TODAY</u>

Hillary Rodham Clinton crushed Barack Obama by more than 2-1 in the West Virginia primary Tuesday—a victory that was surely personally satisfying but came as the Democratic presidential nomination is nearly in the grasp of her rival.

"There are some who have wanted to cut this race short," Clinton told raucous, cheering supporters in Charleston, but she left no doubt she plans to stay in the race through the final contests. "I am more determined than ever to carry on this campaign until everyone has had a chance to make their voices heard," she said, calling herself a stronger candidate in a general election and a better-prepared president.

Obama, who had made just three campaign stops in West Virginia, was campaigning instead in Cape Girardeau, Mo.—a battleground state in the fall—and focusing on presumptive Republican nominee John McCain. "There is a lot of talk these days about how the Democratic party is divided," he said, "but I'm not worried because I know that we'll be able to come together quickly behind a common purpose."

Still, surveys of voters as they left polling places spotlighted Obama's difficulty in winning over white, working-class voters who have been a mainstay of Clinton's support and who dominate the Mountain State's electorate. She won white women by 3-1 and white men by 2-1. Whites without a college degree voted for her by 3-1. Seven of 10 voters said Clinton shared their core values; fewer than half said that of Obama. Race was also a factor: One in five said it was important in their vote. Of those, 85% backed Clinton. A third of Clinton supporters said they would vote for Obama in November if he is nominated. Nearly as many said they would defect to McCain. A quarter said they'd stay home.

—Susan Page

pressure to stay in was immense. She had proven that she would be an extremely tough opponent for Republican candidate John McCain and that she was a formidable debater. All of these compelling reasons kept her in the race.

But in the end, the numbers don't lie. According to national polls, most Americans felt that Hillary Clinton would be a better commander in chief than Barack Obama. But they also felt that he would do a better job of unifying the country. During the Bill Clinton and George W. Bush presidencies, the United States had been extremely divided along party lines. After sixteen years of bitterness between the two parties, Americans were tired of governments that were so partisan nothing got done. Despite Hillary Clinton's many qualifications, Barack Obama came to represent the unity that many voters were looking for.

On June 7, 2008, Hillary Clinton conceded defeat and called for the Democratic Party to come back together. She thanked all of her supporters for believing in her and working so hard on her behalf. She also wholeheartedly gave Barack Obama her full support.

Even though she was admitting defeat, Hillary Clinton managed to find triumph at the conclusion of her campaign. The fact that she had gotten far closer to winning her party's nomination than any other U.S. woman was in itself a win for the country. In her concession speech, she referred to her 18 million supporters.

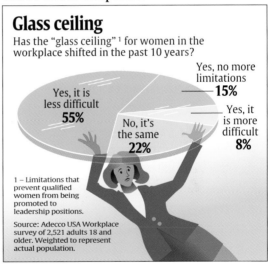

## USA TODAY Snapshots®

### Glass ceiling

Has the "glass ceiling" [1] for women in the workplace shifted in the past 10 years?

Yes, it is less difficult **55%**

No, it's the same **22%**

Yes, no more limitations **15%**

Yes, it is more difficult **8%**

1 – Limitations that prevent qualified women from being promoted to leadership positions.

Source: Adecco USA Workplace survey of 2,521 adults 18 and older. Weighted to represent actual population.

By Jae Yang and Alejandro Gonzalez, USA TODAY, 2008

Although she hadn't broken through the "highest, hardest ceiling" separating the United States and its first woman president, she said that that barrier now had 18 million cracks in it.

**Message of unity:** Hillary spoke at the Democratic National Convention in Denver, Colorado, in August 2008. She talked about uniting the Democratic Party behind the presidential candidate, Barack Obama.

### After the Race

After conceding, Hillary returned to Washington, D.C. Being on the campaign trail had diverted her attention from her work in the Senate. While pursuing the presidency, Hillary had often expressed her concern for the well-being of the nation's economy. She proved her sincerity by proposing the revival of a bill that was used during the Great Depression of the 1930s—the greatest financial crisis the United States had ever faced. The bill, called the Homeowner's Loan Corporation, was designed to help struggling Americans pay their mortgages so they could keep their homes.

While the general election for president was being contested by Barack Obama and John McCain, Clinton experienced a resurgence in popularity. Polls placed her approval rating at a 67 percent. Her endorsement of Obama carried that much more weight with her loyal voters, helping him win the presidency in November 2008. Later that month, the president-elect asked Clinton to serve as his secretary of state. In this role, Clinton would be tasked with tackling some of the United States' and the world's most challenging relationships.

Clinton asked for time to think over the idea. Taking the position of secretary of state would mean sacrificing the Senate seat she had worked so hard to gain. She'd no longer be able personally to push for solutions to issues dear to her heart, such as health-care reform.

Yet in many ways, Clinton was ideal for the post being offered to her. The U.S. secretary of state is the top foreign policy official. Whoever holds this office is essentially the first representative of the United States to the rest of the world. A successful secretary of state needs a firm grasp of foreign affairs. The person needs the ability to negotiate with hostile powers while also upholding U.S. principles

**Obama's nominee:** Obama and Hillary leave a news conference in December 2008 that announced her officially as Obama's nominee for secretary of state. They are followed by *(bottom to top)* Vice President-elect Joe Biden; Defense Secretary Robert Gates; Arizona governor Janet Napolitano, nominee for secretary of Homeland Security; and Eric Holder, attorney general nominee.

and looking out for the nation's best interests abroad. As First Lady, Hillary Clinton had traveled to more than eighty countries and had endeared herself to countless foreign leaders. Throughout her campaign for the presidency, she had demonstrated her keen understanding of the world stage and had highlighted her international experience.

Clinton accepted the job, pending her confirmation by the Senate. By agreeing to join Obama's administration, she demonstrated to the world that although she and the president-elect had sparred with each other for most of 2008, they were united in the best interests of the country.

The confirmation hearings gave senators an opportunity to discuss not only Hillary's knowledge and competence but to question the impact of her husband's foundation on public policy if she was confirmed. In fact, the Obama transition team had met with Bill Clinton to remove any concerns the senators might have. Yet the members of the committee persisted in wanting to make sure his work would not involve hers and that he'd check in with the White House so his efforts would not compromise any U.S. initiatives she was pursuing for the U.S. government. Despite these reservations, the committee voted for confirming her, and the full Senate confirmed her appointment by a vote of 94–2. Hillary stepped into what she described as a "difficult and exciting adventure."

Hillary wanted to foster new ideas at the State Department. Soon after starting her job in 2009, she launched a suggestion box via e-mail for all employees of the State Department and the U.S. Agency for International Development. They can send their ideas directly to her for comment or discussion.

## December 1, 2008

# Clinton's biggest test: How she'll work with Obama

<u>From the Pages of</u>
<u>USA TODAY</u>

She'll bring global star power, a long-standing commitment to improving the status of women and children around the world and muscular promises of military action when U.S. interests are crossed. The question for Hillary Rodham Clinton, slated to be named secretary of State today by President-elect Barack Obama, is whether she can forge the sort of close relationship with a former rival that is crucial to giving the nation's top diplomat the credibility to get things done. "What matters most are two things," says James Lindsay, director of the Robert S. Strauss Center for International Security and Law at the University of Texas-Austin. "One, the secretary of State has to have the president's ear. Two, the president has to have the secretary of State's back."

Clinton is "a tough pragmatist who understands it's a dangerous world out there, who understands it can be necessary at times to use force and at other times to be able to back your diplomacy with the threat of force," says Martin Indyk, a former assistant secretary of State and ambassador to Israel who is close to Clinton. "On the other hand, she has shown a very deep commitment to the causes of human rights, women's rights in particular, and the pursuit of peace and resolution of conflict."

Clinton's public campaigning for Obama during the general election and their private conversations in the four weeks since he won have helped mend fences and begin a budding partnership. Obama strategist David Axelrod now calls Clinton "able, tough, brilliant." Even so, no appointment Obama has considered has generated as much chatter as the choice of the New York senator.

—Susan Page

**On the job:** Hillary shakes hands with Japan's minister of foreign affairs in Tokyo in February 2009. The trip to Asia was her first diplomatic trip after becoming secretary of state.

On January 22, 2009, two days after Barack Obama was sworn in as president of the United States of America, Clinton showed up for her first day at the State Department. Hundreds of State Department employees met her upon her arrival with a resounding burst of applause. Many wondered how she would perform in this challenging position and what approaches she would take when facing the difficulties that lay ahead.

As a mark of her intent, she chose locations in Asia—specifically Japan, China, South Korea, and Indonesia—as her first overseas trip. In so doing, she and the Obama administration signaled that Asia's expanding markets and military might are important to the United States and that the country wants to have influence in the region. She followed up that first overseas visit with trips to the Middle East and Europe. She also made recommendations for persons to appoint as special envoys in some of the worst hot spots, such as Afghanistan and the Middle East.

Although the future is uncertain, Hillary Rodham Clinton's confidence is rock solid. Speaking with diplomats about her new job she said, "This is not going to be easy. . . . But if it weren't hard, someone else could do it."

# SOURCE NOTES

10   Hillary Rodham Clinton, *Living History* (New York: Simon and Schuster, 2003), 9.

10   Gail Sheehy, *Hillary's Choice* (New York: Random House, 1999), 24.

10   Norman King, *A Woman in the White House: The Remarkable Story of Hillary Rodham Clinton* (New York: Birch Lane Press, 1996), 5.

11   Sheehy, *Hillary's Choice*, 24.

11   King, *A Woman in the White House*, 5.

12   Joyce Milton, *The First Partner: Hillary Rodham Clinton* (New York: William Morrow and Company, 1999), 14.

13   Ibid., 25.

13   King, *A Woman in the White House*, 10.

16   Clinton, *Living History*, 24.

19   Sheehy, *Hillary's Choice*, 39.

20   Milton, *The First Partner*, 24.

24   Clinton, *Living History*, 37.

26   Ibid., 38.

27   Hillary Rodham, "Wellesley College 1969 Student Commencement Speech," *Wellesley College*, February 25, 2008, http://www.wellesley.edu/PublicAffairs/Commencement/1969/053169hillary.html (May 6, 2009).

30   Clinton, *Living History*, 52.

30   Sheehy, *Hillary's Choice*, 75.

31   Clinton, *Living History*, 75.

31   Sheehy, *Hillary's Choice*, 82.

34   Clinton, *Living History*, 69.

37   Ibid., 74.

38   King, *A Woman in the White House*, 60.

40   Sheehy, *Hillary's Choice*, 133.

43   Ibid., 196.

44–45   Clinton, *Living History*, 102.

46   Ibid., 105.

46   Ibid., 106.

47   Ibid., 107.

48   Clinton, *Living History*, 109.

64   Patrick E. Tyler, "Hillary Clinton, in China, Details Abuse of Women," *New York Times*, September 6, 1995, http://www.nytimes.com/1995/09/06/world/hillary-clinton-in-china-details-abuse-of

-women.html (May 6, 2009).

64    Hillary Rodham Clinton, *It Takes a Village and Other Lessons Children Teach Us* (New York: Simon and Schuster, 1996), 12.

68–69    Clinton, *Living History*, 341.

71    Ibid., 445.

71    Ibid., 446.

79    Elizabeth Kolbert, "The Student," *New Yorker*, October 13, 2003, http://www.newyorker.com/archive/2003/10/13/031013fa_fact_kolbert (May 6, 2009).

79    Ibid.

83    Ibid.

90    John Roberts, "Hillary Clinton Launches White House Bid: 'I'm In,'" *CNN.com*, January 22, 2007, http://www.cnn.com/2007/POLITICS/01/20/clinton.announcement/index.html (May 6, 2009).

99    *New York Times* transcript, "Hillary Clinton's Pennsylvania Primary Speech," April 22, 2008, http://www.nytimes.com/2008/04/22/us/politics/22text-clinton.html (May 6, 2009).

101    *New York Times* transcript, "Hillary Clinton Endorses Barack Obama," June 7, 2008, http://www.nytimes.com/2008/06/07/us/politics/07text-clinton.html?scp=1&sq=Hillary%20Clinton%20endorses%20Barack%20Obama&st=cse (May 6, 2009).

104    Ed Henry, Ed Hornick, Kristi Keck, and Jamie McIntyre, "Hillary Clinton Endorses Barack Obama," *CNN.com*, December 1, 2008, http://www.cnn.com/2008/POLITICS/12/01/transition.wrap/index.html (May 6, 2009).

106    Anne Flaherty, "Clinton's First Day: Welcomed at State Department," *Huffington Post*, January 22, 2009, http://www.huffingtonpost.com/2009/01/22/obama-tasks-clinton-to-st_n_159936.html (May 6, 2009).

## SELECTED BIBLIOGRAPHY

"About Senator Hillary Rodham Clinton," *Senator Hillary Rodham Clinton*, 2004. http://clinton.senate.gov/about_hrc.html (August 9, 2004).

Clinton, Bill. *My Life*. New York: Knopf, 2004.

Clinton, Hillary Rodham. *It Takes a Village and Other Lessons Children Teach Us*. New York: Simon and Schuster, 1996.

——. *Living History*. New York: Simon and Schuster, 2003.

King, Norman. *A Woman in the White House: The Remarkable Story of Hillary Rodham Clinton*. New York: Birch Lane Press, 1996.

Milton, Joyce. *The First Partner: Hillary Rodham Clinton*. New York: William Morrow and Company, 1999.

Osborne, Claire G., ed. *The Unique Voice of Hillary Rodham Clinton: A Portrait in Her Own Words*. New York: Avon Books, 1997.

Sheehy, Gail. *Hillary's Choice*. New York: Random House, 1999.

## FURTHER READING AND WEBSITES

### Books

Benson, Michael. *Bill Clinton*. Minneapolis: Twenty-First Century Books, 2004.

Freedman, Russell. *Eleanor Roosevelt: A Life of Discovery*. New York: Houghton Mifflin Company, 1997.

Gourley, Catherine. *Gidgets and Women Warriors: Perceptions of Women in the 1950s and 1960s*. Minneapolis: Twenty-First Century Books, 2008.

——. *Ms. and the Material Girls: Perceptions of Women from the 1970s through the 1990s*. Minneapolis: Twenty-First Century Books, 2008.

Levy, Debbie. *The Vietnam War*. Minneapolis: Twenty-First Century Books, 2004.

Morris-Lipsman, Arlene. *Presidential Races: The Battle for Power in the United States*. Minneapolis: Twenty-First Century Books, 2008.

Ryan, Bernard, Jr. *Hillary Rodham Clinton: First Lady and Senator*. New York: Facts on File, 2004.

### Websites

"First Ladies' Gallery"
http://www.whitehouse.gov/history/firstladies
This site offers biographies of every First Lady in U.S. history.

The State Department
http://www.state.gov
This site provides videos and reports of Hillary's travels and meetings as U.S. secretary of state.

# INDEX

## PHOTO ACKNOWLEDGMENTS

The images in this book are used with the permission of: © Jay LaPrete/USA TODAY, p. 1; © Rob Curtis/USA TODAY, pp. 3, 7, 14, 25, 35 (top), 43, 45, 49, 55, 57, 60, 69, 73, 80, 84, 86, 88, 92, 98, 100, 105; AP Photo/Elise Amendola, p. 4; © Jack Gruber/USA TODAY, p. 6; © Tim Boyle/Newsmakers/Getty Images, p. 9; William J. Clinton Presidential Library, pp. 10, 30, 37, 52; Ernest Ricketts, p. 13; AP Photo, p. 16; Maine South High School, pp. 18, 46; © Lee Balterman/Time & Life/Getty Images, p. 21; © Sygma/CORBIS, pp. 26, 32; Michael Marsland/Yale University, p. 28; © David Hume Kennerly/Getty Images, p. 35 (bottom); © Mike Stewart/CORBIS SYGMA, pp. 36, 42; Arkansas Democrat-Gazette, p. 39; © Cynthia Johnson/Time & Life Pictures/Getty Images, p. 44; © Luc Novovitch/Liaison/Getty Images, p. 48; © Les Stone/ZUMA Press, pp. 50, 65; © Luke Frazza/AFP/Getty Images, p. 51; AP Photo/John Duricka, p. 54; AP Photo/Ron Frehm, p. 58; AP Photo/ Doug Mills, p. 59; AP Photo/Greg Gibson, pp. 61, 68 (top); © Barbara Kinney/ White House/Time & Life Pictures/Getty Images, p. 63; © H. Darr Beiser/USA TODAY, p. 66; © Tim Dillon/USA TODAY, pp. 70 (left), 74, 78, 87; © Robert Hanashiro/USA TODAY, p. 70 (right); AP Photo/Kathy Willens, p. 76; © Mark Vergari, The Journal News/USA TODAY, p. 77; AP Photo/Mary Altaffer, p. 82; © Shah Marai/AFP/Getty Images, p. 85; © Scott Olson/Getty Images, p. 90; © Bob Daemmrich/The Image Works, p. 93; AP Photo/The Oklahoman, Steve Sisney, p. 95; © Ricky Flores, The Journal News/USA TODAY, p. 97; © Pat Shannahan/USA TODAY, p. 102; AP Photo/Charles Dharapak, p. 103; © Tomohiro Oshumi-Pool/Getty Images, p. 106.

Front Cover: © Scott Olson/Getty Images.
Back Cover: © Todd Plitt/USA TODAY.

## ABOUT THE AUTHOR

JoAnn Bren Guernsey is the author of several young adult novels and many nonfiction titles. Her work has won several awards, and in 2003, she received a McKnight Artist Fellowship in Prose from the Loft Literary Center. Guernsey lives in Minneapolis, Minnesota.